WALES

WALES

Alison Jenkins

RYDON
PUBLISHING

A Rydon Publishing Book
35 The Quadrant
Hassocks
West Sussex
BN6 8BP
www.rydonpublishing.co.uk
www.rydonpublishing.com

First published by Rydon Publishing in 2020

A CIP catalogue record for this book is available from the British Library.

ISBN: 978-1-910821-32-9

CONTENTS

INTRODUCTION

Wales is a small country but one that has a rich and varied history and, despite its size, has made a multitude of amazing and extraordinary contributions to the rest of the world. A proud, big-hearted nation, with a passion for song, poetry and the arts, for sport, food, fun, humour, an ancient land of myth and legend and curious traditions, and a boundless capacity for diversity and innovation.

Where to start? In the words of our own most famous poet Dylan Thomas '*to begin, at the beginning*', the beginning was in fact a very long time ago, the oldest human remains discovered in Wales date from about 230,000 years ago, and then there's the mysterious 'Red lady of Paviland' a curious 29,000-year-old case of mistaken identity. Welsh pre-history is evidenced by many extraordinary man-made structures such as Bryn Celli Ddu and the Hindwell Enclosure, not to mention the astonishing Welsh contribution to Stonehenge. Wales is bristling with ancient stone circles, burial chambers and much more.

Moving forward in time, learn about the mysterious hill forts − the purpose of which remains unknown − and the hundreds of impressive stone fortifications and castles which bear testament to the Welsh struggle to defend themselves from invaders. Wales boasts many interesting architectural features, from Telford's engineering masterpiece the Pontcysyllte Aqueduct, which is held together with mortar and ox blood, to fairytale follies such as Castell Coch and Portmeirion, and then there's the giant concrete apple of course.

Wales is breathtakingly beautiful, a haven for wildlife with natural wonders aplenty; an astonishing 20 per cent of Wales is designated National

Parkland. Where else in the world can one experience the solitude of the highest mountain peak or the thrill of exploring the deepest cave system, and where indeed can you walk around the entire country on one continuous footpath? Oh yes and there's the glorious rain; if you ever visit Wales, don't forget your raincoat!

Discover how Welsh pioneers and innovators changed the world. Did a Welshman discover America before Columbus, or make a powered flight before the Wright Brothers? Find out about many more unsung heroes and about the Welshman who helped put men on the moon. Wales also has its fair share of famous and infamous people, the heroes and villains of folklore and real life. Who was the first woman to be tried for witchcraft and who was 'Mr Nice'? Did you know that Wales was the world's first industrialized nation and the first ever million pound deal was struck in Cardiff? Learn about Welsh industry from prehistoric copper mines to the black gold that fuelled the industrial revolution. And finally, find out what the Welsh did and do for fun. Which ancient sport was played naked, why Victorian day trippers shared their journeys with the dead, and where one can discover the joys of bog snorkelling!

The following pages contain a selection of lesser known amazing and extraordinary facts that will both amuse and intrigue. Enjoy!

Alison Jenkins
Llanelli, 2020

ARCHAEOLOGY

The history of Wales spans many thousands of years.
Archaeological evidence tells us much about how
ancient communities lived, hunted, worshipped and
showed respect for their dead, suggesting that our
ancestors – while very different from ourselves –
were far from primitive.

A CASE OF MISTAKEN IDENTITY
The Red Lady of Paviland; or was she?

In 1822 William Buckland (1784–1856) a professor of
Geology at Oxford University discovered part of a human
skeleton while on an archaeological dig at Goat's Hole Cave
(also known as Paviland Cave) on the Gower peninsular in
South Wales. The skeleton and decorative bone and shell
artefacts were stained red, leading Buckland to deduce that
the remains belonged to a 'painted lady' of ill repute who
might have been associated with the Romans at a nearby
camp. Buckland was a creationist and refused to believe that
the remains could pre-date the biblical great flood. However,
the red staining was found to have been caused by naturally
occurring red oxide, and recent studies show that the remains
are of a healthy young adult male aged between 25 and 30,
who was buried in the cave approximately 29,000 years ago.
How he died remains a mystery, but the nature of his burial is
indicative of a sophisticated social structure and respect for the
dead. The environment in which this young man lived would

have been very different then, the cave would have overlooked grassy plains that stretched for 96 km (60 miles) before they reached the sea.

Analysis of the bones reveals that our man was partial to a diet of meat, fish and shellfish, evidence that he was a resourceful hunter gatherer. This extraordinary find is thought to be the oldest ceremonial burial site in Western Europe.

PONTNEWYDD CAVE
The story of the 230,000-year-old teeth

The oldest human remains to be found in Wales were uncovered during excavations deep inside Pontnewydd cave in the Elwy Valley in Denbighshire between 1978 and 1995. The nineteen teeth found in the cave are believed to belong to a group of several Neanderthal individuals, adults and children, and are thought to be 230,000 years old. A fragment of an upper jaw containing a worn milk tooth and a permanent molar is thought to be the remains of a child aged 8 or 9. Neanderthals were short in stature, thick set, with heavy jaws, thick ridged brow bones and large teeth. Not a pretty sight! Their branch of the complex human evolutionary tree died out about 36,000 years ago, and while our ancestry is shared, modern humans did not evolve from them. These nomadic people were hunters, evidenced by many stone tools and animal bones found at Pontnewydd, but where they came from is unclear.

QUICK FACTS

At this time it was possible to walk across the English Channel so Neanderthals might have travelled from Europe to hunt, and taken refuge in the cave, or possibly used the caves to bury their dead.

CANTRE'R GWAELOD
(The Lowland Hundred)
An extraordinary testament to climate change

Ancient folklore tells the tale of a kingdom that once existed on a tract of dry land between Ramsey Island and Bardsey Island under the waters of what is now known as Cardigan Bay. According to legend, the flood gates in the dyke that protected the kingdom from the sea were left open

AMAZING FACT

Fossilized tree stumps are all that remains of several forests that once existed around the coastline of Wales, providing evidence of land that has been lost to the sea. Studies at the site in Cardigan Bay show the trees died about 5,500 years ago. In 2019 the low tides and high winds as a result of storm Hannah revealed a prehistoric forest once more.

EXTRAORDINARY FACT

THE LYDSTEP PIG

In 1917 the 6,300-year-old skeleton of a pig was found trapped beneath a fossilized tree trunk in Lydstep Haven near Tenby in Pembrokeshire. Two flint arrowheads found in the beast's neck were undoubtedly the cause of death, providing a clear indication that our Mesolithic man was a hunter. What is unclear is whether this was a failed hunting effort or a ritual sacrifice. More recently in 2010 human footprints of adults and children were found in peat deposits on the beach near to the pig skeleton site. The footprints were deep, suggesting that the group had stood still in one place for a length of time. Perhaps it was the hunting party that had lain in wait for the pig?

by mistake, but who did it is unclear. Cantre'r Gwaelod was consumed by the waves and the kingdom lost. Myths and legends usually have an element of truth and this tale can be seen as evidence of a significant climate change, that is, the end of the ice age and the resulting rise in sea levels that changed the shape of our coastline.

DID YOU KNOW? It is said that the bells of Cantre'r Gwaelod church can still be heard to toll beneath the waves.

A MONUMENTAL NEOLITHIC BUILDING PROJECT
The unsolved mystery of the 'bluestones'

Stonehenge is an impressive prehistoric monument on Salisbury Plain in Wiltshire, comprising two concentric rings of huge standing stones believed to have been constructed during the late Neolithic period, around 2,500 BC. The outer ring is made from local 'sarsen' sandstone and are 4 m (13 ft) tall and weigh about 25 tons, the smaller stones of the inner ring are 'bluestones' from the Preseli hills in Pembrokeshire, which is 240 km (150 miles) west of the site. It is thought that there were originally 42 bluestones each weighing about 2 tons. Why and how the stones were

DID YOU KNOW?

Use of the bluestones is intriguing in that most Neolithic structures used materials sourced from within 16 km (10 miles) of the site.

Stonehenge

transported and exactly who did it is unclear. Was it overland, by water, by glacial movement, extra-terrestrial intervention, magic? It is likely that the stones were physically dragged overland on wooden sledges by teams of extremely sturdy Welshmen; this herculean task would have taken an awfully long time!

THE HINDWELL ENCLOSURE
ANOTHER UNSOLVED ARCHAEOLOGICAL MYSTERY

In 1994, aerial photography revealed the impression of an enormous oval shaped enclosure near Hindwell in Radnorshire, believed to be about 2,700 years old. The scale is astonishing; there are 1,400 equally spaced timber posts, each more than 0.6 m (2 ft) in diameter and probably 6.1 m (20 ft) high marking the perimeter, which measures more than 2 km (1 ¼ miles), the

> **QUICK FACTS**
> The enclosure would have disappeared long before the Romans arrived in Wales.

area covers about 34 hectares. The spaces between the posts were probably filled with timber fences or barriers of some kind. However the exact purpose of the enclosure is unknown but it must have been highly significant to the large community it served when one considers the manpower involved in its construction and the sophisticated organization behind such a large scale project.

Bryn Celli Ddu

EXTRAORDINARY FACT

BRYN CELLI DDU (the mound in the dark grove)

Bryn Celli Ddu, located on the island of Anglesey, is a fine example of a
Neolithic passage tomb that is about 3,500 years old. The passage and
burial chamber lie beneath an earth mound, which is surrounded by
a stone circle. The entrance to the passage aligns with the position of
the sunrise during the Summer Solstice, allowing light to flood into the
chamber illuminating the back wall.

DID YOU KNOW?

A strange stone monolith some 2 m (6 ft 6 in) tall decorated with a swirling continuous pattern on both sides was found buried beneath the chamber floor. It is thought to have been part of the original circular henge that predates the tomb. No one knows what the patterns represent – perhaps an association with the Summer Solstice. A replica of the stone has now been erected inside the tomb.

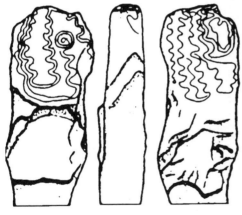

Pattern Stone

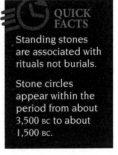

QUICK FACTS

Standing stones are associated with rituals not burials.

Stone circles appear within the period from about 3,500 BC to about 1,500 BC.

ARCHITECTURE

Wales can boast a multitude of architectural masterpieces that span the centuries, including ancient castles and cathedrals, extraordinary feats of engineering, whimsical follies and modern masterpieces plus a very popular giant concrete apple.

QUICK FACTS

• Chepstow Castle is the oldest; building work began in 1067.

• Newly built castles would have been whitewashed on the exterior.

• Strategic placement on rivers or waterways ensured supplies could be delivered by boat.

• More than 100 castles still exist today, some in ruins sadly but many are remarkably well preserved and are most popular with tourists.

• There are more castles per square mile in Wales than any other country in Europe.

• There are three types of castle: Norman, native 'Welsh' castles and Edwardian.

THE CASTLE CAPITAL OF EUROPE
Stone fortifications and the 'iron ring'

The Welsh landscape was once peppered with more than 600 magnificent castles; but why so many? In short, to subjugate the Welsh! The Normans began a gradual but aggressive expansion west into Wales, after the invasion of England in 1066, building fortifications at river crossings and other strategic points. Over the following two centuries, hundreds of impressive stone castles were built to assert dominance over the Welsh. Edward I (1239–1307) continued the trend during the 13th century, constructing his '*Iron Ring*' of imposing fortresses at Conwy, Caernarfon, Beaumaris and Harlech in North Wales. Welsh resistance was eventually overcome.

THE FASTEST CASTLE IN THE WEST!

Caerphilly Castle is the largest castle in Wales and was built between 1268 and 1271 which, even by modern standards is phenomenally quick. The south east tower which sustained considerable damage during 17th century battles between Cromwell and King Charles I, leans precariously at an angle of about 10 degrees, which could be considered a challenge to the Leaning Tower of Pisa which leans at a mere 4 degrees.

Caerphilly Castle

QUICK FACTS

The design of a typical Celtic cross is thought to have appeared during the 7th century and comprises a wheel or ring surrounding the intersection of two perpendicular arms of a standard cross shape, often bearing intricate interwoven carved patterns. There are about 450 examples of stone crosses throughout Wales. An impressive collection of ancient Celtic stones at St Illtyd's Church in LLantwit Major in the Vale of Glamorgan, dates from the 9th and 10th centuries.

EXTRAORDINARY FACT

CASTELL COCH

One might be fooled by the turrets and drawbridge into thinking that the fairy tale castle known as Castell Coch (Red Castle) that overlooks the Taff Valley near Cardiff is many centuries old; it isn't. It is a nineteenth century whimsy in the Gothic Revival Style created by eccentric architect William Burges (1827–1881) albeit upon the site of a 12th century Norman fortification. John Crichton-Stuart, the 3rd Marquess of Bute, a very wealthy man, inherited the castle in 1848, and in 1875 work began to rebuild the castle as his occasional summer residence.

Carreg Cennen

* AMAZING FACT *

THE FARMER WHO PURCHASED A CASTLE BY MISTAKE

In the early 1960s, Gwilym Morris, tenant of 'Castle Farm' near Llandeilo in Carmarthenshire, was given the opportunity by Lord Cawdor, his landlord, to purchase the land he rented. Mr Morris bought the farm and after the sale realized that an error in the legal documents meant that nearby 13th century castle Carreg Cennen had been included in the transaction. Mr Morris refused an offer to buy back the castle, and the castle remains privately owned by the family, managed now by Cadw, Wales' historic environment service.

DID YOU KNOW?

According to legend, whoever is brave enough to spend the night at Tinkinswood Tomb before May Day, St John's Day or Midwinter Day, would become a poet, go insane or die. The first option would be the favourite.

QUICK FACTS

AMAZING ANCIENT SITES

• Pentre Ifan in Pembrokeshire is a 6,000-year-old portal dolmen. Three stone monoliths support an enormous capstone weighing an estimated 16 tons.

• Bryn Cader, a circular cairn in Gwynedd, has been described as resembling a crown of stone thorns. The small circular cairn comprises 15 slender stone slabs, each leaning slightly outward like a crown.

• Gwal-y-Filiast or St Lythans burial chamber is Neolithic dolmen in the Vale of Glamorgan. Three monoliths support a capstone which on Midsummer Eve is said to spin around three times, then the stones bathe in the river.

• Barclodiad y Gawres on Anglesey is a Neolithic chambered tomb which is decorated in the inside with abstract spiral and zig-zag patterns.

• Near Gors Fawr bog in Pembrokeshire stands an impressive circle of 16 standing stones each about a metre high. Some of the stones are dolerite or Bluestones from the nearby Preseli mountains.

• The Tinkinswood tomb in the Vale of Glamorgan is around 6,000 years old and features a colossal capstone measuring 7.3 m × 4.5 m (24 ft × 15 ft) and weighing in at about 40 tons. How a stone of this size was manoeuvred remains a mystery. Excavations at the site have discovered the remains of more than 50 individuals.

• Parc le Breos on the Gower peninsular in Pembrokeshire is an example of the 'Cotswold/ Severn' style of Neolithic burial chambers. A narrow passage leads to four stone lined chambers which would have been covered with huge capstones, but these are now absent. Studies reveal that the tomb was probably in use for several hundred years; the remains of more than 40 people have been found.

• Foel Drygarn is an Iron Age hillfort situated high on a ridge on Preseli Mountains. The impressive site boasts three Bronze Age cairns and the remains of more than 200 circular dwellings.

EXTRAORDINARY FACT

MYSTERIOUS HILL FORTS

More than a thousand hill forts were built in Wales between 2,500−3,000 years ago as the Bronze age drew to a close, possibly as fortified settlements, symbols of power, burial sites, shrines, storage, animal enclosures; the exact purpose remains a mystery. The population of Wales was not great at the time so it is a puzzle as to why so many hill forts were necessary. Some sites would have been difficult to defend due to their size; some had no water supply.

THE SEVERN CROSSING
Free at last!

On the 17th December 2018 charges to cross the M4 and M48 bridges from England into Wales were lifted. It was the first time in more than 800 years that a Severn Estuary crossing had been toll free. The first Severn Bridge between Aust in Monmouthshire and Chepstow in Gloucestershire was opened by the Queen in 1966, replacing the Aust Ferry; a second bridge was opened in 1996. In 1873 the Great Western Railway began to construct the Severn Railway Tunnel. This ambitious project was a little more than 4 miles (7,000 m) long and took 14 years to complete. It held the record for being the longest underwater tunnel in the world for a hundred years, and until the completion of the Channel Tunnel rail link in 2007 was the longest railway tunnel in the UK.

AMAZING FACT

The first reference to a ferry crossing dates from the 12th century, though a passage existed during Roman occupation.

★ AMAZING FACT ★

DYLAN AND DEFOE

The ferry passage across the Severn Estuary between Aust and Beachley was treacherous. During the 18th century writer Daniel Defoe (1660–1731) refused to make the crossing as he was not convinced that the boat would make it. Services were abandoned when the railway tunnel opened in 1886, then in the 1920s the Aust ferry was re-launched. Bob Dylan used the ferry during his 'Judas' tour in 1966. Feinstein's iconic image of Dylan on the jetty was used for Martin Scorsese's documentary about Dylan's life called *No Direction Home*. The first Severn Bridge can be seen while still under construction in the distant background.

QUICK FACTS

The laser sound effects in *Star Wars* (1977) were generated by striking the suspension cables of the first Severn Bridge.

EXTRAORDINARY FACT

The Newport Transporter Bridge, which spans the river Usk in Monmouthshire was opened in 1902, and is one of only six in the world. The bridge can be described as an 'aerial ferry' – a platform, or gondola, is suspended from tracks on a high-level boom, between tall towers on each river bank. Passengers and vehicles could then be hauled from one side to the other. The Transporter featured in *Tiger Bay*, a 1959 crime drama starring Hayley Mills. However, in the movie, Ms Mills boards the gondola in Newport and somehow is transported all the way to Cardiff!

DID YOU KNOW?

The Whiteford Lighthouse at Whiteford Point on the Gower Peninsular was designed and built in 1865. It is the only remaining example of a wave-washed cast iron lighthouse in the British Isles and one of a few worldwide. The light ceased to shine in 1921, and the structure is now derelict, but still a much-loved landmark.

South Stack Lighthouse in Anglesey is the much photographed lighthouse. The rock formations at the site feature on the cover of Roxy Music's 1975 album *Siren*.

South Stack Lighthouse, Anglesey

'*HIGH*'WAYS
Telford's extraordinary achievements

Thomas Telford (1757–1834) was an architect and civil engineer, a builder of canals, roadways and bridges throughout Britain and creator of two of the most extraordinary architectural features of Wales; the Pontcysyllte Aqueduct and the Menai Suspension Bridge.

The Pontcysyllte Aqueduct is a breath-taking 306.9 m (1,007 ft) long, stone and cast iron navigable structure that carries the Llangollen canal at a dizzying height of 39 m (127 ft) above the river Dee in north east Wales. You can cross the 3.6 m (11 ft 10 in) wide aqueduct by canal boat, though passengers are advised to stay below deck, or if you're made of stern stuff you can take the foot path — it's a long way down.

QUICK FACTS

• The Pontcysyllte Aqueduct is a Grade I listed building, a World Heritage site, has 19 arches and is the highest and longest aqueduct in Britain.

• Mortar used in construction contained ox blood; it was thought the ox's strength would be conferred to the bridge.

• The first stones were laid in 1795 and the structure took ten years to complete.

• *Pontcysyllte* means 'bridge that connects'.

• The aqueduct was opened shortly after the Battle of Trafalgar.

DID YOU KNOW?

The Menai Suspension Bridge is mentioned in *Through the Looking Glass* by Lewis Carroll. The White Knight tells Alice that rust could be prevented by boiling the bridge in wine!

The Menai Suspension Bridge completed in 1826, spanned the Menai Straights between the mainland and Anglesey as an alternative to dangerous ferry crossings. Cattle trade with mainland Wales was important to Anglesey, farmers would drive the animals into the water so that they could swim across the strait; a risky practice. Suspension bridges were not a new idea, but an engineering project of this scale was ground breaking. Telford's design comprised two towers, with a span of 176 m (577 ft) suspended by sixteen enormous chain cables. The structure was situated at the narrowest part of the strait, and at more than 30 m (100 ft) high allowed safe passage of tall ships underneath. It was the first suspension bridge designed to carry road traffic, and at the time was the longest bridge in the world with a span of 176 m (579 ft).

Menai Suspension Bridge

THE BIG APPLE
The giant concrete fruit gains Grade II listed building status

The 'Big Apple' is a small kiosk and landmark situated in Mumbles in Glamorgan that has been a joy to children and adults for generations. Tragedy struck in 2009 when the apple was almost demolished by a motorist in a Ford Fiesta. It was repaired and restored to its former glory and was back in business by 2010 providing refreshments to holidaymakers. Grade II Listed Building Status was granted in 2019 as a result of a vigorous campaign by local supporters. The apple shaped concrete kiosk was one of many built in the 1930s in seaside towns across England and Wales as part of a promotional campaign by a drinks brand called 'Cidatone'. There were originally two more in South Wales at Porthcawl and Barry. The Mumbles' 'Big Apple' is now the only surviving example in the UK.

ST DAVID'S
A TINY TOWN HAS BIG ASPIRATIONS

St David's in Pembrokeshire is known as the smallest city in the United Kingdom, with a population of roughly 1,800. During the 16th century, Henry VIII declared that a town could be considered a city if it had a cathedral − St David's has a magnificent example dating from around 1180. However this criterion was abolished in 1888 and St David's city status was lost. City status was not restored until 1994 by special request of Queen Elizabeth II.

DID YOU KNOW?

During the Middle Ages the shrine of St David in St David's Cathedral was considered a highly significant pilgrimage site. In 1123 Pope Calixtus II declared that two pilgrimages to St David's were equal to one to Rome, and three were equivalent to a journey to Jerusalem.

St David's Cathedral

QUICK FACTS

Ffordd Pen Llech in the town of Harlech in North Wales has earned itself the title of 'Steepest street in the world' boasting a gradient of 37.5 per cent at the steepest point, beating Baldwin Street in New Zealand with 35 per cent into second place.

EXTRAORDINARY FACT

Quay House, the smallest house in the United Kingdom is to be found on the quay side in the town of Conwy in North Wales. You can't miss it as it is painted bright red. This tiny 'one up one down' dwelling was built in the 16th century and has a floor area of just 3.05 by 1.8 metres (10 ft by 5 ft 9 in). The last inhabitant of Quay House was fisherman Robert Jones who vacated the property in 1900, he was 190.5 cm (6 ft 3 in) tall and was unable to stand up inside! Quay House is now a popular tourist attraction.

St Trillo's Chapel is the smallest church in Wales and indeed in Britain, seating just 6 people. St Trillo built his cell here during the 6th century, his source of drinking water was a natural spring inside.

PORTMEIRION
ITALIANATE JEWEL OF THE NORTH

Portmeirion, in Gwynedd North Wales, was the brainchild and lifelong project of British architect Sir Clough Williams-Ellis (1883–1978) who coined the phrase, 'Cherish the past, adorn the present and construct for the future'. It was built between 1925 and 1975 in a flamboyant and eclectic Italianate style and is considered to be one of the influences on late 20th century Post-Modernist architecture. Acclaimed American architect Frank Lloyd Wright (1867–1959), proud of his own Welsh heritage, visited Portmeirion in 1956 and was impressed by Clough-Williams ability to combine architectural styles. Portmeirion is a popular tourist destination today.

DID YOU KNOW?

'I am not a number. I am a free man'
The 1960s cult classic television series *The Prisoner* starring Patrick McGoohan was filmed on location in Portmeirion. The titular character known only as 'Number 6' is an ex British Intelligence agent who is abducted and held captive in a strange and mysterious Italianate coastal town referred to as 'The Village', from which there seems no escape.

QUICK FACTS

• *The Great Glass House at the National Botanic Gardens of Wales* Designed by Norman Foster, this amazing glass structure houses more than 1,000 different rare species of plant and is the largest single span greenhouse in the world.

• *Millennium Arts Centre, Cardiff* Also known as the 'Armadillo', is an award winning 21st century national icon, a testament to Wales' passion for the arts. The giant bilingual poem that adorns the front of the building reads 'In these stones horizons sing', then 'Creu Gwir fel Gwydr o Ffwrnais Awen', which means: 'Creating truth like glass from inspiration's furnace.'

★ AMAZING FACT ★

St Fagans National
Museum of History is an
open-air museum near Cardiff
which was first opened in 1948 and
features more than 40 buildings from all over
Wales that have been rescued and reconstructed
to reflect the diversity of Welsh architecture,
and all aspects of Welsh life through the ages.
Buildings include a pig sty, a cockpit and a
toll booth, chapels, a terrace of ironworkers'
cottages, two working mills and much more.
There are plans afoot to open a pub on site. The
Vulcan Hotel opened in 1853 and is a historic
hotel and public house that was located in the
Adamsdown suburb of Cardiff,
South Wales. In 2012 it was
donated to St Fagans, where it
is being reconstructed.

DID YOU KNOW?

In 1997 the Welsh people voted in favour of
a National Assembly for Wales. The 'Senedd'
building opened in 2006 as the home of the
assembly. Traditional Welsh materials such
as slate and oak were used in the building's
construction, together with glass and steel which
reflects a spirit of openness and transparency.
The building is also recognized as being one of
the most environmentally friendly parliamentary
buildings in the world.

CULTURE AND CUSTOMS

The Welsh love a celebration, especially when it involves singing, leeks, daffodils, the wearing of national costume and waving of flags. Wales is fortunate to have Saints and symbols aplenty that are widely recognized as quintessentially 'Welsh'.

SAINT DAVID (late 400s–589)
Patron Saint of Wales. AKA 'David the water drinker'

Though the exact year of St David's birth is unclear, his death is recorded as 1 March 589, known today as St David's Day. According to the legend, St David's mother, St Non, gave birth to her son high on a Pembrokeshire cliff top during a raging storm. The ruins of the tiny chapel of St Non's mark the likely spot and can still be seen today. Many stories tell of miracles performed, the most famous of which took place in a small village called Llanddewi Brefi. While delivering a sermon the audience complained that they couldn't hear. A white dove landed on St David's shoulder and the earth began to rise beneath his feet forming a hill, enabling the crowd to see and hear clearly. St David was a vegetarian and teetotal, he lived a life of austerity existing only on bread and water, hence his nickname 'the water drinker'. He was also known to frequently stand up to his neck in the cold waters of lakes and rivers as a penance.

During his life he travelled widely in Wales and Brittany, teaching and preaching the word of god, establishing churches and monasteries along the way. He urged his followers to practice *ascetism* in pursuit of spiritual fulfilment, a life devoid of sensual pleasure, without meat to eat or beer to drink. This strict diet and lifestyle didn't do David any harm as it is thought that he was more than a hundred years old when he died. St David was buried at the monastery he founded in the Glyn Rhosyn Valley in Pembrokeshire, where St David's cathedral now stands.

THE LEEK
A HUMBLE VEGETABLE WITH MAGICAL POWERS

What other country has a national vegetable? The leek has been associated with Wales for many centuries. The general assumption is that Welsh soldiers were instructed to place a leek on their hats as a means of identification during battle against the Saxons. However the stories vary, as legends often do. Some say that St David led the soldiers into battle, while others say it was King Cadwaladr of Gwynedd, but it's always in a leek field and the Welsh are always victorious. Shakespeare too refers to the wearing of leeks as an ancient Welsh tradition. His character Henry V, who was of Welsh descent, wears a leek with pride claiming 'for I am Welsh, you know, good countryman'. Another character Pistol, who is English, insults the leek on St David's day and was made to eat a raw leek as punishment. It is said that the Romans brought the leek with them, indeed emperor Nero loved a leek, as he said it improved his singing voice. Maybe that is why the Welsh are famed for their voices. Young soldiers in the Welsh Guards still observe the raw leek eating tradition on St David's day – their cap emblem is of course, a leek.

EXTRAORDINARY FACT

The Magical Powers of the Leek

In addition to being the basic ingredient of the famous '*cawl*', leeks have been used over the years to cure colds, purge the blood, heal wounds, alleviate the pain of childbirth, and to protect the bearer from lightning strikes. It is also said that if a young woman sleeps with a leek under her pillow she will dream of her future husband.

THE DAFFODIL

KNOWN AS '*CENHINEN PEDR*' IN WELSH, WHICH MEANS *ST PETERS LEEK*, WHICH IS CONFUSING

The daffodil is a well-known symbol of Wales. While the leek's association with Wales spans centuries, popular use of the daffodil as a national symbol gained momentum only during the 19th century. The hardy daffodil is also associated with St David, the patron saint, and is often seen as a symbol of rebirth, growth, faithfulness and new beginnings, perhaps because it blooms without fail every spring, coincidentally just in time for St David's day. There is a suggestion that David Lloyd George (1863–1945), who was Prime Minister from 1916–22, popularized the wearing of a daffodil on 1 March, perhaps a little more pleasant than a leek to sport in one's buttonhole.

WELSH LOVESPOONS
And they say romance is dead?

The giving of a lovespoon is a romantic Welsh tradition that dates back to the 17th century. A love-struck young man would carve a wooden spoon from a single piece of close-grained wood incorporating various symbols of love to present to his sweetheart as a prelude to courtship. There were no hard and fast rules as to what form the spoon should take – simple heart, locks, keys and other shapes could be combined with linked chains and other intricate patterns, much depended on the ability and imagination of the carver. However, the more intricate the design, the better his romantic chances. The skill of the carver would give the young lady's father an indication of the young man's intentions and also demonstrate the level of his craftsmanship and thus his ability to provide for his daughter and future family. Over the years lovespoons became increasingly ornate and as a result lost their practical use, but instead became treasured possessions and family keepsakes. Sailors would often carve lovespoons featuring anchors and rope twists as gifts for loved ones on their return from long voyages at sea. Today lovespoons are popular gifts for engagements, weddings, anniversaries, birthdays or christenings and of course Valentines' day or indeed Saint Dwynwen's day.

MEANINGS OF CARVED SYMBOLS

Single heart – the universal symbol of romantic love, and says 'My heart belongs to you'.

Double heart – indicates a desire for mutual love.

Celtic cross – marriage or faith.

A wheel, a spade – willingness to work hard to provide for the loved one.

Keys and keyholes – 'the key to my heart', security and contentment.

Locks or a house – my house is yours.

Bells – symbolizes a forthcoming wedding.

Anchor – strength, steadfastness, security.

Trees, leaves, vines – a love that grows.

Flowers – represent courtship.

Trees, leaves or intertwined vines – represents a love that is growing.

Horseshoe – good luck and happiness.

Barley sugar twist – a nautical symbol used by sailors.

Double spoons – represents the loving couple.

Triple spoons – suggests a desire for a family.

Ball in a cage or links in a chain – the number of balls or links represent future offspring.

Diamonds – prosperity and good fortune.

Paisley shape – sometimes used to represent the soul.

QUICK FACTS

• St Fagans National History Museum near Cardiff, has a fine collection of historic Welsh lovespoons, the earliest dated example was made in 1667. It is not clear exactly when the decorative lovespoon tradition began, but it can be assumed that it was much earlier as spoon carving for utilitarian purposes had been a common practice for many years.

SAINT DWYNWEN

PATRON SAINT OF LOVERS (AND SICK ANIMALS) SAINT
DWYNWEN'S DAY IS CELEBRATED IN WALES ON 25 JANUARY

*According to legend, Dwynwen was a daughter of Brychan
Brycheiniog, a 5th century King who lived in Brecon. Though the
details of her story vary, it goes roughly like this. Dwynwen is
described as very beautiful and in love with a young prince called
Maelon. Unfortunately for poor Dwynwen, her father refused to
give consent for their marriage and in her despair she prays for
help. An angel comes to the rescue with a magic potion and the
offer of three wishes. Maelon drinks the potion and is promptly
turned to ice! Dwynwen utilizes her wishes thus; the first that she
be free of Maelon who was then thawed and undoubtedly made a
hasty exit, the second that God may protect all true lovers and the
third that she may remain unmarried. Her experience of heartbreak
prompted Dwynwen to become a nun and dedicate the rest of
her life to helping other lovers. She preached at many churches
throughout Wales before making her way to a life of solitude on a
small island called Llanddwyn which is off the coast of Anglesey.
During the middle ages the church that was built there became an
important shrine, and was a place of pilgrimage for the lovelorn.
The ruins of the church can still be seen today.*

It is said that sacred fish and eels live in the
waters of the holy well on Llanddwyn which
have the power to predict the fortunes of
lovers. Interestingly Dwynwen is also said to
be the patron saint of sick animals.

THE RED DRAGON (*Y Ddraig Goch*)
Mythical beast and quintessential symbol of 'Welshness'

The red dragon's significance and association with Wales has been recognized for centuries, possibly introduced by the Romans. The legendary King Arthur favoured the dragon on his battle standard. The Mabinogion story of *Lludd and Llefelys* tells of fierce battles between red and white dragons. In Merlinic prophecy, the red dragon represents the Welsh and the white dragon the invading Anglo-Saxons. The dragon emblem was used by the Kings of Gwynedd, by Owain Glyndŵr as a symbol of revolt against the English and by Henry VIII to demonstrate his Welsh heritage. The distinctive Welsh flag comprises a central red dragon, *passant*, on a field of white and green; the dragon represents Cadwaladr King of Gwynedd, the green and white, the House of Tudor. Each colour is significant — red for valour

EXTRAORDINARY FACT

The Welsh flag does not feature in the British Union flag. Wales was annexed to England by Edward I (1239–1307), then fully integrated under the 'Acts of Union' 1536 and 1543 by Henry VIII (1491–1547) thus the principality of Wales became a part of the Kingdom of England and Wales. When the union flag was designed in 1606 Wales was represented by default by the cross of St George. The red dragon flag only gained official status as the flag of Wales in 1959.

and bravery, white for peace and honesty, green for joy and hope, and possibly a nod to the leek! Henry VIII used the flag combining Tudor colours and the dragon at the Battle of Bosworth in 1485, and during *The Historia Brittonum* records the use of a symbolic red dragon in 829 AD.

★ AMAZING FACT ★

**HOW WALES
SAVED THE RED
KITE FROM EXTINCTION**
The red kite (*Milvus milvus*) is the
national wildlife symbol of Wales and an
extraordinary conservation success story. Red
Kites were once considered vermin throughout
Britain and at the end of the 19th century they
had been exterminated in England and Scotland.
By the early 20th century the population had
been reduced to a few breeding pairs found only
in the secluded woodlands of mid Wales. Efforts
were made by local conservationists, farmers and
enthusiasts to ensure that nests were protected
from egg hunters, and as a result numbers
gradually began to increase. It took more than
a century of perseverance but today, Wales
can now be proud to be the habitat
to several hundred breeding pairs.

MARI LWYD
A battle of words with a horse skull brings good luck

'*Mari Lwyd*,' which in translation means 'grey mare' is a tradition dating back to the early 1800s and is as extraordinary as they come. Celebrated at Christmas or New Year, the Mari Lwyd costume consists of a horse skull decorated with bells and colourful ribbons, mounted on a pole then covered with a sheet. A person hidden beneath the sheet carries the Mari Lwyd from house to house challenging the householders to a battle of rhyming verses and insults called '*pwnco*' in order to gain access to the house. It is customary to let Mari Lwyd and her mischievous followers into the house eventually in order to drive out evil spirits and afford good luck for the year ahead. Once inside, songs were sung and much food and drink consumed.

EXTRAORDINARY FACT

'Holming' was a rather unpleasant tradition which took place on Boxing Day morning. The last person out of bed was thrashed with a holly branch. Luckily this tradition is no longer observed.

Calan Gaeaf is the name for the first day of winter, observed on 1 November, the day after Nôs Galan Gaeaf, or Hallowe'en. Traditionally, women and children would dance around a fire, then paint their names on stones and leave them around the embers overnight. Everyone would run home quickly for fear of losing their soul to a tailless black sow and a headless woman. If in the morning there was a stone missing then this meant that the person would meet their death within a year. Traditionally, people would avoid churchyards, stiles, and crossroads, since spirits are thought to gather there.

TŶ UNNOS
AN ANCIENT HOUSING CRISIS SOLVED OVERNIGHT

An old tradition known as Tŷ unnos *(one night house) holds that if a dwelling, albeit a temporary one, could be built on common land overnight and a fire lit in the hearth by the following morning then the freehold would belong to the builder. The boundary of the surrounding plot would be determined by how far the builder could throw an axe from each of the four corners of the house. Such dwellings were usually built from readily available materials such as timber and turf with a makeshift thatched roof, a more permanent structure could then be built at leisure. The tradition began in response to an increased demand for housing caused by rapid population growth from the 17th to the early 19th centuries. Poverty combined with restricted land availability led to widespread squatting on common land in rural areas.*

NATIONAL COSTUME

How Welsh traditional dress became a national symbol

During the late 18th and early 19th centuries, visitors to Wales observed that the traditional style of dress worn by women in rural areas to be distinct from that of other areas in the country.

A woollen bedgown was worn with an underskirt and petticoat, a neckerchief, apron and shawl, a red or blue hooded cape, and finally the characteristic tall, shallow brimmed black hat. It was not considered a national costume until the 1830s when Lady Llanover (1802–1896), heiress and wife of Benjamin Hall (1802–1867) ironmaster and industrialist in Gwent, began to promote all things Welsh and the development of a Welsh identity. Popularization of the costume was also in some way an attempt to save the woollen industry as rapid industrialisation was seen as a threat to the agricultural industry and traditional ways of life. The wearing of traditional dress declined throughout the 19th century and today is now worn on St David's day or for special celebrations.

QUICK FACTS

'Big Ben', the bell in the clock tower of the Houses of Parliament in London, was named after Benjamin Hall; his name is inscribed thereon.

JEMIMA'S PITCHFORK
BOLD WELSH LADY SAVES THE NATION

QUICK FACTS

A Welsh hat thought to have belonged to Jemima herself sold for £5,000 ($6,454) at auction in 2019.

Jemima Nicholas (1750–1832) also known as 'Jemima Fawr' (big Jemima) was born in Fishguard, where now a commemorative plaque reads 'The Welsh heroine who boldly marched to meet the French invaders who landed on our shores in 1797'. Jemima rose to fame during the Battle of Fishguard (sometimes referred to as the 'last invasion of Britain') when, armed only with a pitchfork, Jemima rounded up twelve inebriated French soldiers from the surrounding fields, marched them into the town and then locked them up in St Mary's church to ensure that they didn't escape. It seems that after a successful landing, the French troops embarked on a looting spree and discovered a haul of wine obtained from a wrecked Portuguese ship; debilitated by over consumption the invasion collapsed and the French began to negotiate a conditional surrender. Lord Cawdor called their bluff and offered an ultimatum to surrender unconditionally by the following morning or risk attack by his 'superior force' which was in fact only a few hundred British Grenadiers. In the morning the red coated soldiers assembled on Goodwick sands in readiness for battle, but, on the cliff top above them, hundreds of local townsfolk had also gathered to watch the proceedings. From a distance, the women dressed in traditional red cape and tall black hats appeared to the French to be the uniform and tall military headgear of thousands of British Grenadiers. Assuming that they were hopelessly outnumbered, the French surrendered.

DID YOU KNOW?

The Welsh triple harp is seen as the national instrument of Wales, however, it is not Welsh as such but originated in Italy around 1600. The instrument was very popular amongst Welsh musicians living in London during the 18th century.

NICKNAMES
A curious and amusing Welsh tradition

Nicknames are used in order to distinguish between people who have the same surname or forename, usually derived from their appearance, profession, where they live or indeed any other quirky characteristic. For example: Jones/ Evans/Thomas, the milk/the coal/the bread, *Dai Patagonia*, who travelled to Argentina, *Penny* who worked for the gas board, *Sioni Winwns* or Johnny Onions, the bicycle riding Breton onion merchants. This amusing story dates from the 1940s. A young apprentice arrived for his first day at work. The foreman asked his name and the apprentice replied 'David or Dai', the foreman said that they had plenty of men called Dai and he would have to be known as Dai 'something'.

QUICK FACTS

Road signs in Wales are bilingual; Welsh and English.

The apprentice said that he didn't mind what he was called only that it be something 'substantial'. He was known as 'Dai substantial' for the rest of his life!

LLANFAIRPWLLGWYNGYLLGOGERYCHW YRNDROBWLLLLANTYSILIOGOGOGOCH
THE SMALL VILLAGE WITH AN EXTRAORDINARILY LONG NAME

This tongue twister of a place name is commonly abbreviated to Llanfair PG, probably to save time. It means 'St Mary's church in the hollow of the white hazel near to the rapid whirlpool of St Tysilio of the red cave'. Llanfair Pwllgwyngyll is a small village on the island of Anglesey in North Wales, the extended version of the name was devised during the 1860s in an attempt to gain fame by having a railway station with the longest name; and to boost tourism. The name has 58 characters but in fact only 51 letters as 'll' and 'ch' are digraphs, i.e. two letters representing one sound, and therefore treated as single letters. It is the longest place name in Britain and arguably the most unpronounceable. Wales also has numerous place names that contain no vowels and some that have only one syllable like 'Pwll', which are equally difficult to say.

QUICK FACTS

• According to the *Guinness World Records* 2002, Llanfairpwllgwyngyllgogerychwyrndrobwllllant-ysiliogogogoch has the longest URL in the world.

• Science fiction classic film *Barbarella* (1968) uses Llanfairpwllgwyngyllgogerychwyrndrobwllllanty-siliogogogoch, as a secret password.

• Welsh band Super Furry Animals used the name as a title for an E.P. in 1995 adding *'yn a gofod'* at the end, which means 'in space'.

• In the film *The Road to Hong Kong* (1962), the Indian neurologist (Peter Sellers) asks Bob Hope to say the very long place name.

• A Stephen Sondheim and Mary Rodgers song *The Boy from ...* (1966) ends as the titular character moves from his home village of Tacuarembó la Tumba del Fuego Santa Malipas Zacatecas la Junta del Sol y Cruz" to Wales to live in Llanfairpwllgwyngyllgogerychwyrndrobwl-llantysiliogogogoch!

• The first Women's Institute – or WI – meeting was held in Llanfair PG on the 16 September 1951.

CAWL, WELSHCAKES AND BARA BRITH
'Feed me 'til I want no more!'

Food is as important a part of a nation's culture as its anthem, language or customs. However, misnomers abound; there are cakes and bread that are neither, vegetarian sausages and rabbit made of cheese. Wales' many culinary traditions have been enjoyed for centuries, regional and family variations are numerous, and everyone thinks that their version is the best.

Cawl dates back to the 11th century (or even further) and is a national staple if not the national dish of Wales. This hearty stew is made traditionally from lamb but sometimes bacon or beef with leeks, root vegetables and potatoes cooked very slowly over a day or more. Often leftover meat or vegetables would be added throughout the week; repeated boiling improves the flavour!

Welshcakes (*picau ar y maen,* meaning cakes on the stone) are a source of national pride. Not really a cake, but a round flat spiced scone/biscuit hybrid, made with raisins or sultanas and served hot or cold, dusted with sugar or plain, but best eaten warm straight from the bakestone or *planc.*

Bara brith is a loaf containing dried fruit and candied peel which would have been soaked in tea beforehand. The name translates to 'speckled bread' and would have been enjoyed sliced and spread with butter at tea time.

Bara brith

EXTRAORDINARY FACT

BREAD OF HEAVEN

Laverbread is an extraordinary food product, and to be clear, is definitely not bread, which can be a little confusing. It is a traditional delicacy made from laver seaweed which tastes delicious, and smells fresh like the

sea air. The seaweed is first rinsed then boiled for several hours until it resembles a greenish black pulp, and that's it, nothing added and nothing taken away. It can be eaten hot or cold, plain or sometimes rolled in oats, but most often as part of a Welsh breakfast, fried with bacon and cockles. Laverbread is highly nutritious bursting with iron and iodine, one could almost describe it as the 'superfood' of Wales. Richard Burton once described laver bread as 'Welsh caviar'.

Only in Wales could cheese on toast reach iconic status. In an amusing 16th century story, God asks Saint Peter to expel the over-boisterous Welsh from heaven. Saint Peter stands outside the pearly gates shouting 'caws pobi' which means 'toasted cheese'. The Welsh immediately rush outside in search of the tasty snack, whereupon the gates are shut behind them. The dish of savoury melted cheese on toasted bread is first referred to as 'Welsh rabbit' in 1725, seen by some as slightly derogatory, implying that the Welsh were too poor to eat meat. The 'rarebit' term appears later in the 18th century and is most commonly used today.

DID YOU KNOW?

In 1882 two German immigrants, Ivan Levinstein and Otto Isler, established a brewery in Wrexham, North Wales, producing the first Welsh lager made in the traditional Bavarian style. Wrexham Lager was the only lager available on the White Star Line's ill-fated ship *Titanic*.

QUICK FACTS

• Welsh Rarebit day is celebrated on the 3 September.

★ AMAZING FACT ★

ALL HAIL FOR THE ALE!
In 1935 Felinfoel Brewery (est. *c*.1878) in Carmarthenshire became the first brewery outside the USA to market beer in cans. The brewery's founder had interests in local iron and tinplate works so the novel idea was a means to stimulate trade and increase local employment. The problem of a metal 'taint' to the beer, experienced by the Gottfried Kreuger Brewing Company in America, was overcome by coating the inside of the can with wax. The half pint bottle shaped can with a crown cap closure was lighter than a glass container and was therefore a more economical option to send to soldiers based overseas during World War I.

LAUGHARNE
A strange town that has a 700-year-old tradition

Described by Dylan Thomas (1914–1953) in 1934 as 'the strangest town in Wales'. Nestled on the Taff estuary in Carmarthenshire, Laugharne is the only remaining medieval corporation in Wales and one of only a few in the UK. The corporation was established in 1290 by Royal Charter, and was presided over by the Portreeve and a body of aldermen and burgesses, who traditionally would have represented the crown and dealt with all town affairs including civil and land disputes and criminal justice. The duties of the court and Portreeve are largely ceremonial today, although the corporation is a registered charity and acts to promote the welfare of the people of Laugharne. The swearing in ceremony, however, is great fun; the good people of Laugharne enthusiastically uphold the tradition.

QUICK FACTS

• The new Portreeve is sworn in at The Big Court on the first Monday after Michaelmas. He dons the symbol office, a chain of golden cockle shells, and is carried shoulder high on a wooden chair three times around the town hall.

• The new Portreeve then ceremoniously buys a round of beers for the burgesses. Cheers!

• The Common Walk or Beating the Bounds occurs tri-annually on Whit Monday. Townsfolk walk the boundary of the Corporation land, selected victims at various landmarks along on the way are asked to name the place, if they fail, they are turned upside down and beaten three times on the backside.

• The title Portreeve is derived from the words 'port' or sea town, and 'reeve' which means a high ranking administrative official.

DID YOU KNOW?

Dylan Thomas was invited to attend the swearing in ceremony in October 1953, but in a letter to the Portreeve he declined as he was scheduled to travel to the United States. This was his last ever correspondence; he died in November the same year.

Laugharne town hall

WONDERLAND

Wales is a land brimming with wonders that have been created both by Mother Nature and the hands of man and occasional extra-terrestrials! Take a stroll around the entire coast or climb the highest mountain peak and experience the wealth of extraordinary natural beauty.

NATIONAL PARKS
Preserving the natural beauty of Wales

There are three National Parks in Wales – their purpose is to conserve and protect areas of natural beauty, wildlife environments and cultural heritage. Snowdonia boasts 827 square miles of mountains, presided over by Mount Snowdon towering 1,085 m (3,560 ft) above the lakes and glorious wilderness. The Brecon Beacons are a paradise of mountains and undulating terrain with hidden castles, caves and breathtaking waterfalls. Pembrokeshire National Park was the first in Britain to comprise entirely of coastal areas; a haven for beachcombers and birdwatchers alike. The 299 km (186 mile) long Pembrokeshire Coastal Path winds its way around craggy headlands past ancient rock formations and natural stone arches, one can look out to remote islands, lighthouses and explore more than 50 spectacular beaches.

> **QUICK-FACTS**
> The National Parks cover an incredible 20 per cent of the land in Wales.

★ AMAZING FACT ★

STARRY STARRY NIGHT
The entire Brecon Beacons National Park was declared an International Dark Sky Reserve in 2012; the first in Wales. Due to an absence of light pollution, on a clear night stargazers can see the Milky Way and a multitude of shining heavenly bodies. Snowdonia National Park was only the tenth site in the world to gain Dark Sky status, while Pembrokeshire National Park is considered a Dark Sky Discovery site.

DID YOU KNOW?

Wales has 5 Areas of Outstanding Natural beauty, 14 Heritage Coasts, 12 Sites of Specific Scientific Interest and numerous nature reserves and protected conservation areas.

EXTRAORDINARY FACT

The rainfall in Wales is a frequent source of mirth to the non-Welsh, and indeed the Welsh. However, precipitation in Wales is in fact significant, receiving on average 24.64 cm (97 in) of rainfall per year. September is the driest month, while wet weather peaks in June. Snowdonia is the wettest place, while Flintshire is one of the driest. The village of Eglwyswrw, in Cardiganshire, endured rain for 85 consecutive days from October 2015 to January 2016, narrowly failing to beat the record of 89 days set in Scotland in 1923.

THE BROAD HAVEN TRIANGLE
THE WELSH X FILES

In 1977 a series of UFO sightings in Pembrokeshire made national news. Fourteen children from Broad Haven Primary School claimed to have seen a strange craft and a 'spaceman' next to the playing field. The children produced remarkably similar drawings of a cigar shaped craft with a dome, and a silver suited person. Teachers and members of staff also claim to have seen the same 'UFO' and the creature, later, indeed a local hotel owner spotted a saucer shaped craft and two humanoid forms. The phenomena were reported to the Ministry of Defence but investigations were inconclusive. There were numerous extraordinary UFO 'sightings' that year and to this day the phenomenon remains a mystery.

S.O.S. SAVE OUR SANDS
The community that challenged the MOD

Cefn Sidan beach in Pembrey, Carmarthenshire, is a glorious 12-km-long (8 mile) shallow crescent of golden sands punctuated only by a few skeletons of ships that floundered in the treacherous waters in days gone by. However, in 1969 the Ministry of Defence proposed to relocate the gunnery range from Shoeburyness, Essex, to Pembrey, thus denying public access to the beach and extensive woodlands. Local communities formed opposition committees and men, women and children began their fierce campaign to overturn the decision. School children took part in a competition to design banners for the protest marches that followed, an S.O.S. banner was flown from the steeple of Pembrey church, protesters formed human chains to sabotage attempts by the MOD to get the survey and construction process underway, even laying down in front of military vehicles to prevent access to the sands. A petition containing 27,000 signatures was presented to a public inquiry committee, which in due course found that the MOD had failed to consider the full impact that the gunnery range would have on the environment and the local community. The decision was reversed and the protest made history in becoming the first organization to defeat the MOD. Today Cefn Sidan beach and 500 acres of woodland truly remain a natural wonder and one of the South Wales' most popular attractions.

★ AMAZING FACT ★

**THE LONG
WAY ROUND**
The Wales Coast Path was
opened on the 5 May 2012. It is a
continuous 1,400 km (870-mile)
walking route that follows the coastline
of Wales from Chepstow in the south to
Queensferry in the north. Wales is the
first country in the world to have a
dedicated coastal footpath. The path
connects with the Offa's Dyke Path
which runs along the border with
England to create an incredible
1,657 km long (1,030-mile)
round trip of Wales
in its entirety.

QUICK FACTS
Offa's Dyke is thought to
have been constructed by
Offa, who was the Anglo-
Saxon King of Mercia
during the 8th century,
in order to contain the
Welsh, or indeed to keep
the English out!

THE PHENOMENON OF THE 'SINGING SANDS'

If you walk along the sand on Porth Oer beach on the Llyn Peninsula in North Wales on a warm dry day you'll hear the sand 'sing' or 'whistle' beneath your feet. The sand there is largely made of quartz particles which are unusually uniform in shape and size, well rounded and regular so when you walk on them, they rub together making a delightful sound.

QUICK FACTS

• Wales can boast 44 blue flags; a higher concentration per mile than anywhere in Britain.

• Flying the flags are 40 beaches, 3 marinas and one boat tour operator.

• A coast on three sides means that Wales has a lot of beaches – about 490 in fact, and that's only counting the ones with official names, there are numerous coves that aren't really 'beaches' as such.

EXTRAORDINARY FACT

RECORD BREAKERS

The 11 km (7 miles) of smooth hard sand at Pendine in Carmarthenshire has provided an excellent surface for car and motorcycle racing since the 1920s. On the 25 September 1924 Malcolm Campbell (1885–1948) used the beach to secure the World Land Speed Record at 235.22 km/h (146.16 mph) in his Sunbeam car 'The Blue Bird'. Between 1924 and 1927 two more attempts were made by Campbell and two by Wrexham born J.G. Parry-Thomas (1884–1927) in his car 'Babs'. Tragically Parry-Thomas died when Babs crashed during his attempt to break Campbell's new record of 280.38 kmh (174.22 mph), he was the first man to be killed in pursuit of the Land Speed Record.

The Blue Bird

ISLAND LIFE
An offshore haven for wildlife

The Pembrokeshire islands are breathtakingly beautiful; a veritable natural wonder. Isolation from the mainland together with the absence of natural predatory mammals allows numerous species of wildlife to flourish, particularly ground nesting birds. The waters around the island are a perfect breeding ground for seal, dolphin and porpoise. In spring the islands are bursting with colour, carpeted with bluebells and red campion. The five main islands are Ramsey, Skokholm, Skomer, Grassholm and Caldey, which is the only inhabited island. Wales was not colonized by the Vikings due to fierce resistance from the Welsh kings, however, a few small settlements were established in Pembrokeshire, many place names are of Viking origin. In Norse, Skokholm means 'wooded island' while Skomer is derived from 'Skalmey' which means 'cleft island'.

EXTRAORDINARY FACT

THE SKOMER VOLE

As the name would suggest, this elusive little vole is endemic to the island of Skomer. It is unclear how the vole arrived there – perhaps from a boat visiting the island, but they have been in residence long enough to become genetically different from a common mainland bank vole.

QUICK FACTS

• Skomer and Skokholm provide a home for the largest colony of colourful Puffins in southern Britain, upward of 22,000 birds.

• Skomer supports half the world's population of the Manx Shearwater, that's about 300,000 pairs.

• Rare storm Petrels breed on Skokholm, thought to be around 5,000 birds, 20 per cent of Europe's breeding population.

• Grassholm's gannetry is one of the most significant in the world, up to 39,000 breeding pairs which represent about 10 per cent of the world's gannet population.

• Skomer supports a huge colony of guillemot, while smaller populations can be seen on Skokholm and Grassholm.

• Toads, frogs, newts, lizards and slow worms also thrive on these offshore islands.

• Caldey is now a popular tourist attraction and is the only inhabited island. Caldey monastery has been inhabited by monks since the 12th century, while pirates and smugglers are also said to have used the island as a refuge.

DID YOU KNOW?

THE LEGEND OF ST JUSTINIAN

St Justinian is said to have been a Breton Nobleman who established a strict holy community on Ramsey Island in about 550. However, the monks grew tired of the rigid regime and consequently beheaded him. Undeterred, St Justinian picked up his head, put it under his arm and walked across the Ramsey sound to the mainland, where he was buried in a small chapel that now bears his name.

QUICK FACTS

• Sir Edmund Hillary used Snowdon as a training ground in preparation for his ascent of Mount Everest in 1953.

• In 2014 Stuart Kett used his nose to roll a Brussels sprout to the top of Snowdon in aid of Macmillan Cancer Support. It took 4 days and 22 sprouts!

EXTRAORDINARY FACT

The Llangernyw Yew in St Digain's churchyard in Llangernyw village is thought to be more than 4,000 years old. An ancient spirit who can prophesy death is said to inhabit the tree.

THE SEVEN WONDERS OF WALES

An English visitor to North Wales during the 18th century penned a rhyme to describe the points of interest that made his trip so memorable.

'Pistyll Rhaeadr and
Wrexham Steeple
Snowdon's mountain without
its people
Overton yew tree,
St Winefride's well
Llangollen bridge, and
Gresford bells.'

PISTYLL RHAEADR At 72 m (240 ft) Pistyll Rhaeadr near Llanrhaeadr-ym-Mochant in Powys is the highest waterfall in Britain and is a Site of Specific Scientific Interest. A hike to the top via the footpath is rewarded with splendid views of the surrounding mountain landscape.

WREXHAM STEEPLE Not actually a steeple, but a 15th century 41.15 m (135 ft) high tower attached to St Giles' Church in Wrexham. The earliest reference to the church is 1220, and in 1330 severe gales destroyed the steeple. Legend holds that it was punishment for having market day on Sunday. The church and tower were rebuilt and completed in 1509. The grave of Elihu Yale, founder of Yale College in the United States, can be found in the graveyard.

SNOWDON'S MOUNTAIN The jewel in Snowdonia's crown, Mount Snowdon stands more than 1,085 m (3,560 ft) high and is the highest mountain in Wales and England. Ascend to the summit by foot or train; during the 18th century our traveller and poet might have taken a donkey ride to the top.

OVERTON YEW TREE 21 Yew trees stand in the churchyard of St Mary the Virgin in Overton-on-Dee in Clwyd. One tree was planted by the Queen in 1992, the other 20 are believed to be between 1,500 and 2,000 years old.

ST WINEFRIDE'S WELL For more than 1,000 years pilgrims have travelled to St Winefride's well in Holywell, Flintshire in order to take the miraculously curative waters. Richard the Lionheart is said to have made the pilgrimage in 1189. Legend tells the tale of how St Winifred tried to escape a seducer who caught her and cut off her head. A spring formed on the spot where her head fell.

LLANGOLLEN BRIDGE Is a fine example of medieval architecture; the graceful sandstone arches were built in 1500 to replace the previous structure constructed in 1345.

GRESFORD BELLS The bells of All Saints Church in Wrexham are famed for their purity of tone and the fact that an ingenious mechanism means that all 8 bells can be rung at once by just one person. The same bells have been in use since the 1700s.

THE GREAT DELUGE
A tidal surge or ancient Tsunami?

On the 30 January 1607 a huge body of water swept up the Bristol Channel drowning more than 2,000 people and destroying farms and livestock, houses and villages. The devastation stretched for an estimated 51,800 ha (200 sq miles) from Laugharne in Carmarthenshire to Chepstow in Monmouthshire. A commemorative brass plaque on the wall inside the church in Goldcliff near Newport marks the height

of the flood water some 91 cm (3 ft) above the ground. Accounts state that the morning had been sunny, but that the sea had receded before the wave rushed back faster than a man could run, and that the water resembled 'dazzling, fiery mountains'. Current theorists suggest that the wave was in fact a Tsunami, evidenced by the characteristic displacement of large boulders and the erosion of rock along the coastline and unusual sand deposits that are only caused by a very high velocity flow of water.

QUICK FACTS
SURF'S UP

• The Severn Estuary is known for its tidal surges; the Severn Bore is an extraordinary natural phenomenon. Bores occur twice a day on about 130 days in the year, but are most significant when following the new and full moon. The tidal range is one of highest in the world.

• When a large bore is anticipated, surfers ride the wave which can be up to 7.5 m (25 ft) high and travel at speeds of about 13–15 knots (24–27 mph).

• The Severn bore was first surfed in 1955 by Jack Churchill, a World War II veteran and surfing enthusiast, who was known to have killed an enemy soldier using a long bow.

★ AMAZING FACT ★

THE DISAPPEARING LAKE

Pant y Llyn Lake in South Wales is the only '*turlough*' lake in Britain. It has no inlet or outflow waterways and is fed by groundwater rising from the limestone below. Turlough lakes mysteriously fill in autumn and drain themselves in summer. There are, of course, an abundance of folk tales and ghost stories associated with this unique water feature. About two hundred years ago quarrymen are said to have found 13 skeletons in a nearby cave, which were believed to have been the remains of a Welsh soldier called Owain Lawgoch (*c.* 1330−1378) and his men. According to legend, the soldiers slept in the cave, awaiting the call to save Wales from the enemy.

EXTRAORDINARY FACT

TAFF'S WELL AND THE GHOST OF THE GREY LADY

Taff's Well is situated near Cardiff and is the only thermal spring in Wales. It was popular during the 18th and 19th centuries due to the healing properties of the water. The ghost of a lady in grey robes is said to frequent the well. It is said that she approached a man who was collecting water from the well, asking him to hold onto her hands tightly. Unfortunately, the gentleman's grip was not sufficient to save her from the waters and she complained that she would have to remain a ghost for another hundred years.

GOING UNDERGROUND

Farmers discover hidden subterranean labyrinth

Wales has a history of mining that stretches back for centuries and before that natural caves provided refuge for hunter gatherers, so it's no surprise that there's as much to explore below ground as there is on the surface. However, the attraction of 'going underground' for fun is not a modern phenomenon. In 1912 brothers Tommy and Jeff Morgan discovered the entrance to the 'Dan yr Ogof' cave system on their farm in Powys. The brothers spent many years exploring the 16 km (10 miles) of underground passageways and caves with nothing more than candles to illuminate the darkness and a coracle to cross stretches of water. Tommy Morgan was able to produce photographs of the underground caverns which in turn attracted attention from the public. The brothers began leading tours underground and over the years built up a thriving tourist business. Today Wales has numerous cave systems that can be explored, but some require expert knowledge, specialized equipment and an abundance of steely courage – not just a guide book and a torch. Dan yr Ogof caves are part of the National Showcaves Centre of Wales and are situated in the Brecon Beacons National Park.

QUICK FACTS

• The Morgan brothers were not the first to venture into the underground labyrinth; numerous animal bones together with the skeletons of 42 individuals have been found in one of the underground chambers dating back 3,000 years.

• The Dan yr Ogof cave complex was voted the greatest natural wonder of Britain in 2005.

• Ogof Ffynnon Ddu, which means 'Cave of the Black Spring', was discovered in 1946 and, at 300 m (984 ft) deep, is the deepest cave in Britain.

EXTRAORDINARY FACT

Named after 'Sultan' the last pit pony, who was retired in 1999, the giant earth sculpture situated in the valleys of South Wales took three years to build and was completed in 1999 by artist Mick Petts. It is 200 m (656 ft) long and took 60,000 tons of earth and coal shale to construct. The work is a tribute to the hardworking pit ponies used in the coal industry from the 18th to the end of the 20th century. From the air he can be seen galloping freely with legs outstretched, a far cry from the reality of their harsh and restricted life underground in the darkness of the coal pits.

AMAZING FACT

'THE SIZE OF WALES'

Wales is frequently used as a unit of measurement in order to make comparisons or estimate size or scale, for example areas of deforestation, icebergs, asteroids, the size of lakes and indeed other countries.
Land area of Wales is about 20,779 km^2 8,023 (8,023 sq miles).
1 x Wales = 2 million rugby pitches (2 million hectares).
316 x Wales = Amazon rainforest.

MOVERS AND SHAKERS

The extraordinary stories of Welsh pioneers who explored unknown lands, inventors who pushed the boundaries of science and technology, great thinkers and mathematicians who provided answers to life's big questions and those innovative and resourceful people who came up with brilliant ideas that shaped the world as we know it.

THE LEGEND OF MADOC
Did a Welshman discover America before Columbus?

M adoc, or Madog ap Owain, a 12th century prince, is said to have discovered the Americas more than three hundred years before Christopher Columbus made his discovery in 1492. According to the legend, Madoc set sail westward from Llandrillo in Gwynedd, in 1170, then returned the following year to recruit more adventurous folk to join him in the newly discovered lands. He sailed once more across the Atlantic and was never seen again. It is said that Madoc and his followers integrated with the local Native Americans giving rise to many Welsh speaking communities in the Midwest. Thomas Jefferson (1743–1826) 3rd president of the United States who spoke, read and wrote Welsh, also believed the Madoc legend, instructing an expedition to find Madoc's mysterious Welsh speaking descendants. Indeed, Queen Elizabeth I (1550–1603) was most inclined to support the Madoc legend for political reasons. If indeed he got there before Columbus then she could legally claim possession of the Americas for England.

QUICK FACTS

• The Mandan people, who are a Native American tribe, are known to use bull boats which bear a remarkable similarity to the Welsh Coracle.

• While the legend cannot be proved, Prince Madoc was indeed the son of Owain Gwynedd (*c.* 1100–1170) an important ruler in Wales from 1137 until his death. Madoc is said to have ventured west in order to escape bitter family disputes regarding succession after his father's death.

• The Daughters of the American Revolution erected a controversial plaque at Fort Morgan in 1953

which read '*In memory of Prince Madoc a Welsh explorer who landed on the shores of Mobile Bay in 1170 and left behind with the Indians the Welsh language*'. The Alabama Parks service removed the plaque in 2008; it has never been reinstated.

DID YOU KNOW?

There is a compelling theory that 'America' was derived from the name of Welshman Richard ap Meryk, anglicised to Richard Amerike or Ameryk (1445–1503). He was a merchant; a Royal customs officer and it is thought that he was the principle financier of John Cabot's exploratory voyage to North America in 1497. Thus the new lands discovered bear his name as a token of gratitude for his sponsorship.

EXTRAORDINARY FACT

Sir Henry Morton Stanley (1841–1904) born in Denbigh, was a journalist and explorer who was known for his expeditions in central Africa, his search for the source of the Nile and finding the missing missionary and explorer David Livingstone. When Stanley located Livingstone, he said 'Dr Livingstone, I presume?'. A phrase that is probably better known than Stanley himself!

QUICK FACTS

The first Welsh person to officially settle in America was one Howell Powell from Brecon. He began his journey west in 1642, and made his home in Virginia.

THE FLYING WELSHMAN
Who flew first, Bill or the Wright Brothers?

In 1894 Inventor William (Bill) Frost (1848–1935) from Saundersfoot in Pembrokeshire patented a flying machine called the *Frost Airship Glider*. The machine was a powered glider-airship hybrid,

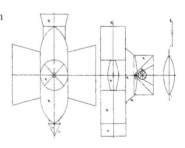

having both a hydrogen cylinder on top plus propellers. According to eyewitness accounts Mr Frost did indeed fly his machine in September 1896, preceding the much-publicized Wright Brothers flight in 1903. The craft flew about 457 m (500 yards) but was damaged by a tree while attempting to clear a hedge, then, before repairs could be made, a storm blew in and destroyed the craft. Unfortunately no official records were made of the flight, but stories of the man 'who flew' are plentiful and are etched in the memories of local families.

★ AMAZING FACT ★

On the 23 June 1942 Luftwaffe pilot Oberleutnant Armin Faber landed his Focke-Wulf 190A fighter plane at RAF Pembrey, Carmarthenshire, thinking it was France. The duty pilot, Sergeant Jeffreys, grabbed a pistol and captured the bewildered enemy airman. This was an amazing stroke of luck as the RAF now had an example of Hitler's formidable fighting machine which at the time was able to outperform the Spitfire. There were indeed daring plans afoot to try and steal one from an enemy airfield. The RAF learned much from the captured plane, facilitating development of the Spitfire Mk IX. The new plane's superior performance in the air shifted the balance of power in Britain's favour, undoubtedly influencing the outcome of World War II.

DID YOU KNOW?

Mr Frost offered the patent for his invention to the Secretary of State for War. The offer was declined as at that time the nation did not intend to use aircraft as a weapon of war. Mr Frost's achievement was never recognized; the patent lapsed as he was unable to afford the renewal fee.

EXTRAORDINARY FACT

Test pilot Brian Trubshaw (1921–2001) was born in Liverpool, but grew up in Llanelli, Carmarthenshire. He piloted Concorde, the world's first supersonic passenger airliner, on its maiden flight on the 9 April 1969. After a safe landing Trubshaw described the experience as 'wizard'.

On the 18 June 1928 Amelia Earhart became the first woman to 'fly' across the Atlantic. The flight began in Newfoundland and ended its journey in Burry Port, Carmarthenshire. However, despite the accolade, she was in fact only a passenger, but did pilot her own plane across the Atlantic later in her aviation career.

CQD
One legged radio enthusiast picks up famous distress signal

On April 15 1912, radio enthusiast Artie Moore (1887–1949) aged 26, from Gelligroes Mill in Monmouthshire, picked up a faint distress signal on a home-made receiver. The young man had lost a leg in a childhood accident and during his convalescence become fascinated by radio communications. The signal had been transmitted in Morse code from RMS *Titanic*; the ship had struck an iceberg in the North Atlantic and was sinking fast. The first of a series of desperate messages read '*CQD* Titanic *41.44N 50.24W*'; CQD was the standard distress code however the newer SOS code was used in subsequent messages. Artie informed the local police who dismissed his claims as nonsense as it was thought that the *Titanic* was unsinkable (and Artie was known as quite an eccentric character). Two days later the newspapers confirmed the *Titanic*'s fate and also that the new SOS code had been used in the transmissions, thus confirming Artie's story. This extraordinary tale came to the attention of inventor Guglielmo Marconi who offered Artie employment in his new communications company.

EXTRAORDINARY FACT ·

'ARE YOU READY'

On the 13 May 1897 Italian wireless communications pioneer Guglielmo Marconi transmitted the first radio signal across open water from Lavernock Point in the Vale of Glamorgan to Flat Holm Island 5.6 km (3.5 miles) out in the Bristol Channel. After a few failed attempts the first message in Morse code read, 'ARE YOU READY' followed by 'CAN YOU HEAR ME'; the response was 'YES LOUD AND CLEAR'. The paper recording slip from this first ground-breaking communication can be seen at the National Museum of Wales.

Physicist Edward George 'Taffy' Bowen (1911–1991) from Swansea is recognized for playing a crucial part in the development of radar during World War II. Bowen pioneered airborne radar systems, which would facilitate air interception, and air to surface detection of enemy ships and submarines.

Scientist Joan Elizabeth Curran (1916–1999) also from Swansea, was involved in 'Operation Window', and invented '*chaff*', a clever countermeasure technique that disrupted enemy radar.

AMAZING FACT

THE EAGLE HAS LANDED

In 1969 Neil Armstrong and Buzz Aldrin made history by walking on the moon, but behind the scenes at NASA control centre, unsung hero Tecwyn Roberts (1925–1988), an aeronautical engineer from Anglesey, was the brain that helped make it happen. He created the 'Deep Space Communications Network' which comprised a chain of huge satellite dishes installed around the globe that would maintain communication and data transmission between the Apollo 8 space craft and the control centre as the earth rotated.

EXTRAORDINARY FACT

PATAGONIA

In 1865 more than 150 Welsh pioneers – men, women and children – boarded the clipper 'Mimosa', setting sail from Liverpool and bound for Patagonia, Argentina, in search of a new life. Their intention was to free themselves from restrictive English influence at home in order to establish a Welsh speaking community Y Wladfa, ('The Colony'), where they could celebrate their non-conformist faith, and follow Welsh traditions and culture. The settlers landed at a natural harbour on the coast of Chubut Province in Patagonia, which they renamed Porth Madryn, now called Puerto Madryn. However, the environment was inhospitable and the first settlers struggled to survive; but persevere they did and after the Central Chubut Railway was opened in 1888, the new colony began to thrive.

QUICK FACTS

• Y *Wladfa* has its own anthem, *Gwlad Newydd y Cymru* ('The New Country of the Welsh') sung to the tune of the traditional Welsh anthem.

• It is estimated that Patagonia is home to around 50,000 people with Welsh heritage, indeed it is said that 5,000 still speak Welsh, albeit 'Patagonia Welsh'.

• Since the 1880s the towns of Gaiman and Trelew in Chubut Province has held a bi-annual Eisteddfod, a celebration of music poetry and performance in the Welsh, Spanish and English languages.

QUICK FACTS

MORE INVENTIONS

• In 1794 Philip Vaughan, an ironmaster, patented the design for the ball bearing. Vaughan's design placed iron balls inside the axle assembly of horse drawn carriages in order to reduce friction between the wheel and the axle thus allowing free rotation of the carriage wheels.

• Edwin Stevens (1905–1995) from Panteg, Monmouthshire, designed the first wearable electronic hearing aid. One of his devices was worn by Winston Churchill.

• In 1965 Donald Davies (1924–2000) a computer scientist from Treorchy, Glamorgan, developed packet switching, a vital concept involved in data communication and computer networks. Where would the internet be without it?

• Isaac Roberts (1829–1904) engineer and amateur astronomer, pioneered deep space photography.

• During clinical trials of a new treatment for angina in Merthyr Tydfil in 1989, volunteers described erectile stimulation as a side effect. This discovery led to the development of 'Viagra'.

THE STEPNEY SPARE WHEEL
Llanelli siblings' novel idea transforms early motoring

In the early days of motoring, cars were not fitted with a 'spare' wheel as such, so in the unfortunate event of a flat tyre the driver had the laborious task of removing, repairing then replacing the wheel and tyre assembly before continuing their journey. However, in 1904 businessmen Thomas Morris Davies and his brother Walter, of Llanelli, patented a clever solution; a spoke-less wheel rim already fitted with an inflated tyre. The rim and tyre could be fitted to the wheel and damaged tyre with adjustable clamps, as a temporary 'fix' in order to get the driver home. The idea was a great success resulting in the formation of the Stepney Spare Motor Wheel Company Ltd in 1906, and the opening of the Stepney Wheel Works in Llanelli to meet increasing demand. By 1909 all London taxis were using 'Stepneys', and indeed the Davies brothers' practical invention was soon in use worldwide.

QUICK FACTS

• The term 'Stepney' is still used today when referring to a spare wheel in India, Bangladesh, Malta and Brazil. Amusingly, in Deli, the term is also applied to an affable staff member who is not of much practical use.

• The Stepney Wheel was displaced when replaceable road wheels came into usage soon after World War I ended.

The Stepney spare wheel

SIR PRYCE PRYCE-JONES
Pioneer of mail-order shopping and the inventor of the 'Euklisia Rug'

Pryce Pryce-Jones (1834–1920) from Newtown in Powys, ran a drapery store supplying locally produced Welsh flannel. During the 1860s, and keen to expand his business, Pryce-Jones took advantage of the new railways systems and improved postal services to promote his services in isolated rural areas. He distributed a catalogue advertising his woollen products, enabling customers to choose and order what they required; the items could then be delivered by post or rail. Business prospered and soon Pryce-Jones was exporting Welsh flannel to Australia and the Americas.

QUICK FACTS

Pryce Pryce-Jones was knighted by Queen Victoria in 1887.

DID YOU KNOW?

In 1876 Pryce-Jones patented the 'Euklisia Rug' the first version of what we now know as the sleeping bag. It was in fact more like a folded woollen rug which could be fastened to form a pocket in which to sleep and keep warm. Records show that this novel item was distributed worldwide – he is said to have sold 60,000 to the Russian army. They were used also by the British army, by civilian missionaries in Africa and pioneers in Australia.

ROBERT RECORDE (*c*.1510–1558)
Parallel lines save time

Physician and mathematician Robert Recorde was born in Tenby, Pembrokeshire. He studied and taught at both Oxford and Cambridge Universities before moving to London in 1547 to practice medicine. He was the author of many influential books on mathematics and algebra and is credited as being the first to use the (+) symbol in a publication and inventing the equals (=) symbol. In his book entitled *The Whetstone of Witte*, 1557, he suggested that a pair of horizontal parallel lines of the same length be used in calculations instead of the tedious repetition of 'is equal to'. In Recorde's own words 'because noe 2 thynges can be moare equalle'.

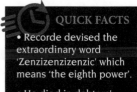

QUICK FACTS

• Recorde devised the extraordinary word 'Zenzizenzizenzic' which means 'the eighth power'.

• He died in debtors' prison in 1558.

DID YOU KNOW?

Alfred Russel Wallace (1823–1931) explorer, naturalist, geographer, anthropologist and biologist from Llanbadoc, Monmouthshire, published an essay on Natural Selection in 1858, pioneering the theory of evolution, one year before friend and colleague Charles Darwin produced his seminal paper *On the Origin of Species*. Wallace was one of the leading 19th century theorists, but unfortunately did not receive the same recognition as Darwin for his contribution to evolutionary science.

★ AMAZING FACT ★

AS EASY AS PI
William Jones (1675–1749)
from Anglesey was a mathematician
known for his use of the symbol (π) pi,
in order to represent the ratio of the
circumference of a circle in relation to
its diameter. Previously, approximations
such as 22/7 or 355/113 had been used.
He suggested that the use of a symbol to
represent an ideal that could be approached
but never reached, since the *exact*
proportion could not be expressed
in numbers. The symbol π first
appears in 1706 in Jones' work
'*Synopsis Palmariorum
Matheseos*'.

Grove cell

EXTRAORDINARY FACT

WILLIAM ROBERT GROVE (1811–1896)

In 1838 the Swansea born scientist published the paper 'O*n a new Voltaic
Combination*', the following year he developed the 'Grove voltaic cell' a
two-fluid hydrogen fuel cell or, put more simply, a battery. The clever
device comprised separate porous ceramic cells containing zinc and dilute
sulphuric acid, and platinum and concentrated nitric acid; the resulting
chemical reaction produced electricity. He used his platinum zinc battery
to produce electric light for one of his lectures on experimental philosophy
at The London Institute during the 1840s. Grove was ahead of his time, a
forward thinking pioneer of fuel cell technology and energy conservation
who in the midst of the Industrial Revolution which relied on coal and
steam, saw electricity as the future. One can only image what our world
would be like if more attention had been paid to his invention.

ART, LITERATURE AND LANGUAGE

Explore the land of song and poetry, of ancient myth and legend, a land with a unique blend of bilingual literature and a passion for the creative and performing arts that spans the centuries, a land that charms and confuses with a language that is one of the oldest in Europe.

LAND OF SONG
Hymns, arias and male voice choirs

Music and song has been a part of Welsh culture for centuries, it runs in the blood – even the lilting Welsh accent sounds like singing! A quote from the 1941 classic movie *How Green was My Valley* sums it up: 'Singing is in my people as sight is in the eye'. The tradition was consolidated during the Eisteddfod in the 12th century, a celebration of music, song poetry and Welsh culture. The dawning of the industrial revolution in the 18th century brought not only employment and prosperity, but a new sense of community within the rapidly expanding industrial towns. Choral

QUICK FACTS

• The song *Sosban Fach* is usually sung in Welsh though there have been several English variations to the chorus, for example 'who beat the All Blacks' or 'who beat the Wallabies' ... but good old 'Sosban Fach' in reference to rugby triumphs. The song has been adopted as a national rugby anthem and is particularly associated with Llanelli and the tinplate industry.

- Hen Wlad Fy Nhadau or 'Old Land of My Fathers' has been the unofficial national anthem of Wales since 1905. Composed by father and son Evan and James James from Pontypridd. The original title was Glan Rhondda or 'Banks of the Rhondda'.
- Tom Jones' rendition of Delilah has arguably reached anthemic status in the rugby grounds of Wales, alongside traditional classic Sosban Fach of course.

singing as a form of worship in the numerous non-conformist chapels provided a respite from everyday hardships and created a sense of solidarity. Male voice choirs, formed in the working men's clubs, remain a feature of Welsh culture. None but a heart hewn from granite could fail to be moved by a rousing rendition of a Welsh hymn, or a heartbreaking love song like *Myfanwy*. Even if you don't speak Welsh!

SOSBAN FACH
WELSH FOLK SONG ABOUT A LITTLE SAUCEPAN, THAT ALWAYS BRINGS A TEAR TO THE EYE

The well-known nonsense song **Sosban Fach** *or 'Little Saucepan' was first heard in the music halls and inns of popular Llanwrtyd Wells during the mid-1890s. Composed by one Talog Williams from Dowlais, but inspired by a verse written by Richard Davies (AKA* **Mynyddog**) *a poet, singer and Eisteddfod conductor in 1873, as part of another song entitled* **Rheolau yr**

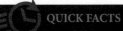

QUICK FACTS
Spillers Record Shop in
Cardiff was established
in 1894 by Henry Spiller
and is known to be the
oldest record shop in
the world.

*Aelwyd or 'rules of the home'. It tells a tale
of a housewife struggling to manage boiling
saucepans of varying sizes, a crying baby, a
child with an injured finger, a poorly servant,
an aggressive cat, combined with a resounding
chorus about little Dai the soldier whose shirt
tail is hanging out. This simple song never fails
to arouse deep emotions, and a tear or two.*

COFIWCH DRYWERYN
Graffiti makes a statement

The iconic *Cofiwch Dryweryn* mural which means
'remember Tryweryn' was painted in the 1960s by Welsh
Nationalist, author and journalist, Meic Stevens on the walls
of a ruined cottage in Llanrhystud, in Ceredigion, as a protest
against the decision to flood the Tryweryn valley and the

MERLIN'S TOWN
During the late 1970s or early 80s graffiti mysteriously
appeared along a row of derelict cottages in the market town of
Carmarthen, Carmarthenshire, which is said to be the birthplace
of legendary wizard Merlin. The graffiti stated 'This is Merlin's
town', then 'This is Merlin's House', then 'Merlin is probably
in the Cooper's Arms'. Sadly the cottages, the graffiti and the
Cooper's Arms are long gone. It is unclear where Merlin calls in
for a pint these days.

★ AMAZING FACT ★

In 2019 the iconic mural was defaced with the word 'Elvis' prompting outcry and an extraordinary public response. Dozens of *Cofiwch Dryweryn* murals popped up all over Wales and indeed as far afield as Chicago and Ohio in the USA in protest. The mural has been vandalized and reinstated many times over the years and is the subject of continuing debate.

farming community of Capel Celyn in order to create the Llyn Celyn reservoir for Liverpool City Council. Tryweryn was one of many villages in Wales to be lost in this way, inflaming nationalist views that the Welsh way of life, the language and culture was under threat.

QUICK FACTS

BANKSY

In December 2018, artist Banksy paid a visit to Port Talbot, leaving behind a mural known as 'Season's Greetings', painted on the corner of a steelworker's garage. On one side a young boy is seen catching falling snowflakes on his tongue, the other side another image shows the harsh reality, the 'snow' is falling ash from a rubbish bin in flames. The image was intended to draw attention to the world's air pollution crisis. In 2019 the artwork was purchased by an art dealer and relocated to a gallery in the town.

EXTRAORDINARY FACT

ELVIS ROCK

The 'Elvis' rock is a well-known piece of graffiti, painted on a rock next to the A44 that runs through Powys. Created in 1962 the graffiti read 'Elis', a gesture of support for Plaid Cymru candidate Islwyn Ffowc Elis. However, the word was mysteriously changed to 'Elvis' soon after. The work has undergone several reincarnations over the years including 'LUFT' and 'JESUS' but now reads 'ELVIS' once more. An intriguing and incongruous sight to behold nestled in the Welsh landscape.

THE MABINOGION
Medieval literary masterpiece inspires modern fantasy genre

M odern fantasy genre has given us *The Lord of the Rings* and *Game of Thrones* to name but two, yet in the middle ages they had *The Mabinogion*. The exact dates are disputed but it is generally thought that the works were compiled during the 11th–13th centuries, drawing from numerous tales previously recounted orally. These enthralling tales of Celtic Mythology filled with magic spells and romance, bloody battles, heroic deeds and mythical beasts, Arthurian legend and more are regarded as the earliest works of prose in Britain. The collection comprises 11 tales

QUICK FACTS

• The first Welsh language Bible was published in 1588, translated from English by Bishop William Morgan (1545–1604) from Penmachno in Conwy. It is considered a crucial event in Welsh language history.

• The 13th century manuscript known as *The Black Book of Carmarthen*, owing to the colour of its binding is believed to be the earliest example of a text written in entirely in Welsh. The text consists largely of 9th–12th century poetry.

featured in two manuscripts *The White Book of Rhydderch* (1300–1325) and *The Red Book of Hergest* (1375–1425) which formed into four main groups or branches known as the Mabinogi, plus seven independent stories that are related to legends of Arthur and his knights or tales of romance and traditional folklore.

The Four branches of the *Mabinogi* are linked by a central character '*Pryderi*'.

Pwyll the prince of Dyfed becomes King of the Underworld.
Branwen a Queen is avenged.
Manawydan Pryderi is enchanted then imprisoned.
Math a bloody battle then Lord Gwynedd transforms his nephews into beasts.

LADY CHARLOTTE GUEST (1812–1895)

English aristocrat and wife of Welsh industrialist and iron master John Josiah, Guest was a leading supporter of the Welsh culture and language. She was a talented linguist and is best known for the complete translation into English and subsequent publication of *The Mabinogion* in 1840.

QUICK FACTS

Lady Guest mistakenly thought that 'Mabinogion' was plural for 'Mabinogi', so strictly speaking the title is incorrect.

THE TREACHERY OF THE BLUE BOOKS

The education report that caused a national outrage

In 1847 the British Government commissioned an inquiry into the state of education in Wales in response to MP William Williams' request that more resources be made available to assist the learning of English in Wales. The report, in the form of three large blue bound volumes, caused outrage throughout Wales. Though many inadequacies had been revealed, the report also portrayed the Welsh as backward and immoral people, whose development was hindered by the Welsh language and the practice of non-conformity. The initial hostile response eventually gave way to a widespread belief that social improvement could only be achieved through adoption and use of the English language. By 1901

QUICK FACTS

• There are 29 letters in the Welsh alphabet. 'J' has been included; where would the Jones' be without it!

• There are 8 double letters or digraphs which count as one, ll, ch, dd, ff, ng, ph, rh, th.

• The alphabet contains no 'K' 'Q' 'X' or 'Z'.

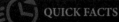

DID YOU KNOW?

THE WELSH NOT

The 'Welsh Not' was a wooden label bearing the letters W. N. used in Welsh schools during the 19th century to deter children from using the Welsh language. The 'Not' was issued to the first child heard speaking Welsh in class and they would have to wear it around their neck until it was passed to the next offender. The process continued until the end of the school day; the last child bearing the 'Not' often received severe punishment.

less than half the Welsh population spoke Welsh, today it is around 19 per cent; but that number is growing.

QUICK FACTS

The Welsh Language Act 1967 afforded some rights for the Welsh language to be used in legal proceedings. It was not until 1993 that Welsh was afforded equal status to English.

THE VOICELESS ALVEOLAR LATERAL FRICATIVE
A QUICK LESSON IN 'LL'

Welsh is one of the oldest languages in Europe, beautiful and expressive, peppered with strange sounds, and those ubiquitous double letters. Some are quite straight forward like 'ch' as in 'loch', 'dd' as in 'other', but let's get straight to the 'll' sound, or the 'voiceless alveolar lateral fricative' and how to do it.

Position the tip of the tongue on the gum behind the front teeth to form a silent 'l', now gently expel air from each side of the mouth, bringing the sides of the tongue up towards the back teeth a little as you do so. It does take a bit of practice.

EXTRAORDINARY FACT

Here are just a few of the many wonderful Welsh words that are better explained through personal experience rather than translation. 'Hiraeth' is a sense of intense 'longing' or 'missing', similar to homesickness. Not easily explained but when you feel it you'll know. 'Cwtch', a proper Welsh hug or cuddle, can also mean a cubby hole, or 'cwtchy' can be used to describe something comfortable and cosy, like a woolly sweater or blanket, or a warm bed or squashy chair. 'Hwyl' is a feeling of motivation and emotional enthusiasm. And finally, where in the world can 'Ear' 'Hear' and 'Here', sound the same i.e. 'yer'! Easily distinguishable by the Welsh, but non-Welsh struggle!

QUICK FACTS

• Roald Dahl (1916–1990) world famous novelist, children's story writer and one-time fighter pilot, was born in Cardiff.

• Bernice Rubens also from Cardiff was the first woman ever to win the Booker Prize for literature with her novel *Elected Member* in 1970.

• Dafydd ap Gwilym was a 14th century poet who wrote about life, love, sex and nature in an amusing and often risqué style. One poem tells how he attended church only to watch the beautiful young ladies.

• Ellis Evans (1887–1917) was a soldier and Welsh language poet. 'Hedd Wyn' was his bardic name. Tragically Evans was killed in action at Passchendaele in 1917 but was posthumously awarded the bard's chair at the National Eisteddfod that year.

• Philologist and author J.R.R. Tolkien (1892–1973) is thought to have used the Welsh language as inspiration for the fictional languages used in his books.

• A Welsh palindrome 'Llad dafad ddall', means to kill a blind ewe.

ART UNDERGROUND
World War II subterranean hiding place

In 1940, as the threat of Nazi invasion was growing, urgent measures were required in order to prevent the precious artworks of the National Gallery from falling into enemy hands. Winston Churchill (1874–1965) said, '*hide them in caves and cellars, but not one picture shall leave this land*'. The vast caverns situated hundreds of feet underground at the disused Manod slate mine near Blaenau Ffestiniog in Snowdonia were chosen as the hiding place. The remote site was considered safe and most importantly, impervious to bomb damage.

EXTRAORDINARY FACT

A PASSION FOR ART

Churchgoing, teetotal siblings Gwendoline (1882–1951) and Margaret (1884–1963) Davies from Plas Dinam in Montgomeryshire, lived relatively sheltered lives but shared a burning passion for art. The sisters inherited a vast fortune from their grandfather, industrialist David Davies, however their Methodist upbringing taught them a sense of social responsibility and to use their wealth wisely. In 1908 while touring Europe, they began what was to become one of the greatest private art collections of the 20th century. The collection is best known for its French Impressionist and Post-Impressionist paintings, including Rodin, Renoir, Monet, Cezanne, Van Gogh to name but a few, but also contains artworks from the Botticelli workshop and many paintings by Welsh artist Augustus John.

Air-conditioned containers to house the treasures were specially constructed underground, and throughout the following year all the artworks were transported from London to Wales by rail and road. The entire collection remained hidden underground for four years.

QUICK FACTS

After their deaths the sisters' impressive collection of 260 works of art were bequeathed to the National Museum of Wales.

DID YOU KNOW?

In 1920 the Davies sisters bought Gregynog Hall in Montgomeryshire in order to establish a centre for arts and crafts and music. The Gregynog Press, set up in 1923, published works in English and Welsh.

QUICK FACTS

A giant painting of Leonardo da Vinci's *Mona Lisa* was unveiled at a shopping centre in Wrexham in 2009. The combined effort of local community groups, the work comprised of 82, 1 × 3 m (3.2 × 9.8 ft) separate pieces.

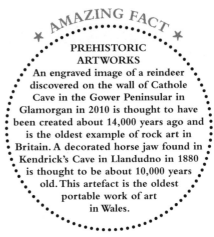

★ AMAZING FACT ★

PREHISTORIC ARTWORKS

An engraved image of a reindeer discovered on the wall of Cathole Cave in the Gower Peninsular in Glamorgan in 2010 is thought to have been created about 14,000 years ago and is the oldest example of rock art in Britain. A decorated horse jaw found in Kendrick's Cave in Llandudno in 1880 is thought to be about 10,000 years old. This artefact is the oldest portable work of art in Wales.

FAMOUS LAST WORDS
'I've had 18 straight whiskies. I think that's the record'

Dylan Marlais Thomas was born on the 27 October 1914 in Cwmdonkin Drive, Swansea. He died aged just 39 on the 9 November 1953 in a New York hospital following a drinking binge. The subsequent post-mortem revealed pneumonia as the likely cause of death, not the preceding whiskies. His last words have become part of the legend that surrounds the turbulent life of Wales' most famous writer and poet. Thomas worked as a reporter for a local newspaper before his focus turned to poetry. Works published while he was still a teenager gained much attention from the literary world and during the 1930s he moved to London to pursue his career, where his reputation as a writer and also a heavy drinker grew. He once said 'I hold a beast, an angel, and a madman in me'. Despite the excesses of his personal life he produced masterpieces such as *Do Not Go Gentle Into That Good Night*, *Fern Hill*, *A Child's Christmas in Wales* and his celebrated BBC radio play for 'Play for Voices' *Under Milkwood*. He met his wife Caitlin in London and they married in 1937 and eventually settled in the small coastal town of Laugharne, in Carmarthenshire. Tourists and lovers of Dylan's work can visit the boat house that was his home and the famous writing shed overlooking the bay where he worked.

DID YOU KNOW?

Dylan Thomas' work can be described as quintessentially 'Welsh', but he wrote only in English.

QUICK FACTS

• There is some debate as to whether 'Llareggub', the fictional village featured in *Under Milkwood* is Laugharne or New Quay in Pembrokeshire. Sitters on the fence would say it's a bit of both, but natives of each town are keen to claim the accolade.

• In *Under Milkwood* we listen to the dreams, desires, hopes and fears of the inhabitants of the fictional village of 'Llareggub'. Now try saying 'Llareggub' backwards!

EXTRAORDINARY FACT

THE LOST MANUSCRIPT

In 1953 Dylan Thomas lost the manuscript for the radio play *Under Milkwood* in London while on a pub crawl. The play, overseen by Douglas Cleverdon, had been commissioned by the BBC in the 1940s but the manuscript, which comprised a scruffy bundle of handwritten notes and type-script pages, was not delivered by Dylan until October 1953, only days before he was due to travel to America on which would be his last tour. Cleverdon is said to have retraced Dylan's steps, eventually finding the missing manuscript in a pub in Soho.

SALEM
The devil is in the detail

Salem is a watercolour created in 1908 by Sydney Curnow Vosper (1866–1942) and is one of the most famous Welsh paintings. The image depicts a typical scene of worship in Capel Salem, a Baptist chapel in Pentre Gwynfryn, Gwynedd. It is also said to be a reference to the sin of vanity as the central character wears an uncommonly bright shawl; an image of the Devil's face is said to be hidden within its folds. Vosper 'staged' the scene in the chapel using real life characters and one tailor's dummy, all dressed in traditional costume; the central figure was one Mrs Siân Owen, aged 71 at the time. It took Vosper some time to complete the painting, and the chapel elders were uncomfortable holding services in the presence of the dummy, so, she was removed every Saturday night before the meeting on Sunday.

Vosper denied including an image of the Devil in Mrs Owen's shawl, but he admitted adding a ghostly face in the church window.

The clock in the painting reads a few minutes past 10, meaning that Mrs Owen is late! It is said that this was to draw attention to her colourful shawl.

Welsh hats were no longer fashionable by the 1900s and Vosper could only find one such hat which he used for all his models.

The popularity of the image in the early 20th century was the result of a promotion by Sunlight soap. Reproductions of the famous image could be obtained if enough tokens from bars of soap were collected.

Vosper named the dummy 'Leusa Jones'.

AUGUSTUS JOHN (1878–1961)
TALENTED AND ECCENTRIC 'KING OF BOHEMIA'

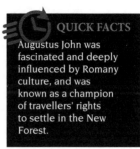

QUICK FACTS

Augustus John was fascinated and deeply influenced by Romany culture, and was known as a champion of travellers' rights to settle in the New Forest.

Born in Tenby, Pembrokeshire, Augustus John is regarded as Wales' most famous artist, known initially for his drawings and etchings, he was widely recognized as Britain's leading portrait artist during the 1920s. A severe head injury sustained in a childhood accident, and the extended period of convalescence, is thought to have stimulated John's adventurous nature, his creativity and artistic expression. An exponent of Post Impressionism, his work has been compared to that of Gauguin and Matisse. His eccentric lifestyle and flamboyant appearance earned him the title 'The King of Bohemia'. Augustus John created the famous portrait of a young Dylan Thomas c. 1937–38. Augustus and Dylan met at The Fitzroy Tavern in London in the mid-1930s. It was Augustus who introduced Dylan to Caitlin Macnamara, who would become his wife in 1937. Other subjects include: David Lloyd George, Winston Churchill, T.E Lawrence, James Joyce, George Bernard Shaw and Tallulah Bankhead.

DID YOU KNOW?

Andrew Vicari (1932–2016), Port Talbot born portrait artist of the rich and famous, was once hailed as Britain's most wealthy painter. He became a millionaire by painting portraits of Saudi Arabian Kings. Vicari called himself 'king of painters' and 'painter of kings'.

NATIONAL EISTEDDFOD OF WALES

An ancient celebration of Welsh culture reinvented by a literary forger

The Eisteddfod is a competitive festival of literature, poetry, music and performance, now conducted entirely in the Welsh language, and held annually during August. The first recorded Eisteddfod took place in 1176 when Rhys ap Gruffydd (1132–1197) invited poets and musicians from all over Wales to perform at a cultural tournament at his court in Cardigan. An elaborate chair was awarded to the most accomplished performer in each discipline. Several Eisteddfodau were held over the following few centuries, and the prized chair has become a traditional symbol. However in Primrose Hill, London in 1792 eccentric Welshman Edward Williams (1747–1826) AKA *Iolo Morganwg* (his bardic name) began a revival, creating the 'Gorsedd of the Bards of the Isle of Britain' in order to promote Celtic culture and heritage. The organization has been closely linked with the Eisteddfod since 1819 and is largely responsible for the elaborate Gorsedd Rites involved in the festival. The first modern Eisteddfod was held in Aberdare in 1861.

EXTRAORDINARY FACT

Iolo Morganwg was an influential poet, antiquarian, collector of medieval Welsh literature, and literary forger. After his death it became apparent that he had forged many ancient texts, despite this however, many of his forgeries are now as well known as the original works.

QUICK FACTS

• *Eisteddfod*, loosely translated into English means 'session', *eistedd* means 'to sit' and *bod* means 'to be'.

• Members of the Gorsedd of the Bards are called druids, their rank is denoted by white, blue or green robes. The leader or Archdruid is elected to conduct Eisteddfod ceremonies for a term of three years.

• After the revival in the 1860s until 1950, Eisteddfodau were largely conducted in English.

• Since 1947, Llangollen has played host to the *International Eisteddfod*, which is an annual celebration of music that attracts artists and performers from around the globe.

• The 'Awen' is a neo-druidic symbol attributed to Iolo Morganwg, and is commonly associated with Eisteddfodau.

• Famous druids (and honorary druids) include the Queen, Winston Churchill, actors Ioan Griffiths and Matthew Rhys and former Archbishop of Canterbury Rowan Williams.

The 'Awen' symbol

DRUIDS

CURSES AND HUMAN SACRIFICE!

Aside from the pageantry of the Eisteddfodau, many myths and legends surround the ancient druids; their curious history stretches back for millennia. Druids were recognized in ancient Celtic culture as powerful spiritual leaders, law keepers, teachers and philosophers, who respected nature and followed natural cycles, who had the power to cure and curse. Though the druids were forbidden from keeping written records, Roman texts contain many references to their practices including rather gory human sacrifice as punishment for criminal acts. While the Romans had pretty much occupied southern

England, they continued to meet with pockets of resistance from southern Welsh tribes the Silures and Ordovices and the Demetae in the north. In 57 AD general Suetonius Paulinus decided to try his luck on the island of Anglesey, which was thought to have been an important druidic site and seat of learning. Roman historian Tacitus (56 AD–120 AD) gives a vivid account of terrified Roman soldiers, faced with hordes of wild haired men and women bearing flaming torches and issuing spine chilling curses at them from across the water. However, the Romans summoned courage, crossed the Menai Straits and mercilessly slaughtered everyone that they could lay their hands on, then burned the bodies. Spiritual leadership crushed, the Welsh lost heart and the rest, as they say, is history.

HALL OF FAME

There are numerous famous and infamous faces, places, and indeed objects and animals that hail from Wales. Read on to learn about Kings and Princes, political giants and stars of the silver screen, heroes and criminals that feature both in legend and folklore and in real life.

GWYR–Y–BWELLI–BACH
The people with the little hatchets

During the 19th century a notorious band of 'wreckers' would light beacons on the shore and hillsides in order to lure ships off course to their doom on the sandbanks between Burry Port and Pembrey in Carmarthenshire. On the 21 November 1829 the ship *La Jeune Emma* met such a fate, amongst those aboard were Napoleon Bonaparte's 11 year old niece Adeline Coquelin and her father. All but a few of the ship's crew were drowned. The hatchet men proceeded to loot the ship, and

⋆ AMAZING FACT ⋆

• **Sir Henry Morgan (1635–1688)** of Llanrumney, infamous privateer and pirate who operated on the waters of the Caribbean, eventually became a wealthy and respected plantation owner and deputy Governor of Jamaica.

• **Bartholomew Roberts (1682–1722) AKA** *Black Bart* earned the reputation as one of the most successful pirates, having captured more than 400 ships on the waters of the Caribbean and North Africa from 1719 until his death at sea in 1722. Robert Louis Stevenson mentions him in his novel *Treasure Island*.

it is believed that they hacked off the young girls' fingers in order to remove her rings. Adeline, her father, and several crew members were buried in St Illtyd's churchyard in Pembrey.

THE RED BANDITS OF MAWDDWY
THE TERRORS OF MID WALES

During the 16th century the Mawddwy area in mid Wales, on the edge of the Welsh Marches, was a lawless and dangerous place terrorized by a ruthless gang of flame haired highwaymen and robbers called 'The Red Bandits'. They ransacked houses and farms, stole livestock and possessions indiscriminately, prompting terrified householders to lodge sharp scythes in their chimneys to impale any bandits who tried to gain entry. On the 12 October 1555 the bandits brutally murdered the Sheriff of Merioneth, Baron Lewis Owen, who had launched a fierce campaign to enforce the law and bring order to Mawddwy. Many Red Bandits were subsequently captured and hanged, thus ending their reign of terror.

Thomas Jones AKA *Twm Siôn Cati*, born around 1530 in Tregaron, Cardiganshire was a popular folk hero – a 'Welsh Robin Hood'. He was a thief and a clever conman who used his quick wits and cunning to outsmart his wealthy victims. Tales of his daring exploits are plentiful, however he is thought to have changed his ways in later life and become rather respectable.

Siôn Cwilt, elusive smuggler, earned his reputation on the remote beaches of Ceredigion during the 18th century. His nickname '*Cwilt*' is thought to have derived from his penchant for wearing colourful cloaks, or perhaps a reference to the Welsh word '*gwyllt*', meaning 'wild'. Constantly pursued by the authorities, but never captured.

William Owen (1717–1747) notorious smuggler, privateer and vicious cut throat killer, was said to have produced an autobiographical manuscript, detailing his exploits while he languished in prison awaiting his execution in 1747.

GELERT
13th century canine hero killed in error

According to legend, Gelert was the favourite hound of Llewellyn the Great (1173–1240) a powerful king who is believed to have ruled Wales for 45 years. Llewellyn returned from hunting only to find his baby son missing from his cradle, the nursery in disarray and Gelert's jaws dripping with blood. Assuming the worst, Llewellyn thrust his sword through the dog's heart, whereupon he heard the child's cries from beneath the upturned cradle. Llewellyn discovered a dead wolf beside the unharmed child, killed by his brave dog Gelert. Filled with remorse, he ceremoniously buried the dog, and it is said that the King never smiled again.

THE BLACK CAT OF KIDWELLY
A symbol of salvation in a plague town

In 1349 The Black Death arrived in Wales. It is estimated that during the ravages of the first year, a quarter of the population was lost. The Welsh believed that the disease was the wrath of God or a manifestation of evil. Kidwelly, a small town in Carmarthenshire is proud to have the image of a black cat as part of its coat of arms and official seal. According to legend, the famous black cat was the first creature to be seen alive after the town succumbed to the disease. The black cat was henceforth regarded as a symbol of salvation and deliverance.

QUICK FACTS

'*Corgi*' is a Welsh word that means 'dwarf dog'.

★ AMAZING FACT ★

'Swansea Jack' was a black retriever who lived in the North Dock area of Swansea in the early 1930s, famed for rescuing a total of 27 people from drowning. Jack received numerous awards for his acts of bravery before he died in 1937. In 2000 a memorial was erected in Jack's honour near Swansea's St Helen's Rugby Ground.

WALES AND THE SILVER SCREEN
Haggar's 'bioscope' and the arrival of the 'talkies'

William Haggar (1851–1915) was one of the early pioneers of Welsh cinema. In 1892 he introduced his 'Bioscope', which was a travelling film show that he would use to make a very good living in the music halls and fairgrounds across Wales. He began making his own films depicting everyday life in Wales in 1901. By the early 20th century, filmmaking began to gain pace as an art form, with hundreds of cinemas springing up all over Wales, and so it rapidly became the most popular form of entertainment. The first 'talkie' film to be set in Wales was James Whales' *The Old*

Dark House (1932), *Proud Valley* (1940) starring Paul Robeson, was set and filmed in the coal fields of South Wales, but *How Green was my Valley* (1940) while famous for the portrayal of Welsh life, starred only one Welsh actor and was filmed in the USA. In 1935 a film documenting the life in a slate quarry in Blaenau Ffestiniog called *Y Chwarelwr* ('The Quarryman'), was the first film to be made in the Welsh language.

QUICK FACTS

• Brynmawr Market Hall Cinema, in Ebbw Vale, is Wales' oldest cinema and has been showing films since 1911.

• La Charrette cinema is a 23 seated venue inside a disused railway carriage once situated in a back garden in Gorseinon, Swansea. It is now at the Heritage Centre, Gower.

• Sol Cinema, housed in a 1970s caravan, is possibly the smallest cinema in the world, having just 8 seats. It is solar powered and fully mobile.

THE LIFE OF BRIAN
Actress turned Mayor lifts 30 year film ban

Monty Python's Life of Brian (1979) the controversial biblical satire, caused worldwide outrage and was banned in many US states, in Ireland and numerous towns across the UK. Welsh actress Sue Jones-Davies played revolutionary Judith Iscariot, but in 2008–9 she took on a new role as Mayor of Aberystwyth. A charity screening of the film was thwarted by the fact that a ban imposed in 1980 was still in place. Mayor Jones lifted the ban.

Kidwelly Castle in Carmarthenshire appears in the opening sequence of *Monty Python and the Holy Grail* (1975). It is said that the fragile remains of an ancient wooden mazer bowl, known as the 'Nanteos Cup', held at the Library of Wales, is in fact the Holy Grail.

Wales' world-famous acting talent includes: Ivor Novello, Ray Milland, Richard Burton, Stanley Baker, Rachel Roberts, Hugh Griffith, Anthony Hopkins, Timothy Dalton, Christian Bale, Catherine Zeta Jones, Rhys Ifans, Mathew Rhys, Ioan Gruffudd and Michael Sheen.

★ AMAZING FACT ★

• *Carry on up the Khyber* (1968) was filmed in Snowdonia.
• *Twin Town* (1997) a black comedy crime drama was filmed entirely in Swansea.
• *Harry Potter and The Deathly Hallows Part 1* (2010) and *2* (2011), and *Robin Hood* (2010), *Snow White and the Huntsman* (2012) all feature beaches in Pembrokeshire.

Ivor Novello

HYWEL DDA (880–948)
Benevolent lawman

'Hywel Dda', or 'Hywel the Good', reigned over much of Wales from 942 until his death and was known as a compassionate leader who chose peaceful negotiation over violent conflict. He codified a sophisticated and comprehensive law system based on common sense approaches to crime as an alternative to capital punishment. For example, murder, assault, or severe bodily harm were dealt with by a system of compensation based on the social status of the victim and the severity of the crime. Women were treated fairly, especially in matters concerning division of property or wealth in the event of divorce or separation. In short Hywel Dda was a pretty good guy; if slightly ahead of his time.

QUICK FACTS

Hywel Dda made a pilgrimage to Rome in 928 AD, the first Welsh ruler to do so, he was also the first to issue his own coins.

EXTRAORDINARY FACT

KING ARTHUR

Geoffrey of Monmouth's *The History of the Kings of Britain* (*c.* 1136) features Arthur, the heroic leader who defended the realm against the Saxon hordes during the 5th and 6th centuries. Though solid written evidence from this period are scarce, Geoffrey managed to produce Arthur, the legendary figure of Merlin the Wizard, the Knights of the Round Table, beautiful Lady Guinevere, Camelot and much more. It is more likely that Arthur is a composite hero, based on many leaders who fought against the invaders. However, the legend endures and is known worldwide; fact or fiction it is an awfully good story!

It seems that cheese was an important commodity in the time of Hywel Dda and worthy of its own clause in the law. A wife owned the cheese while it was still soaking in brine, it only became the property of a husband when it was removed from the brine. Useful for settling arguments when it came to divorce!

OWAIN GLYNDŴR (1359–1415)
GUERRILLA WARRIOR WITH A MASTER PLAN

Owain Glyndŵr was a wealthy, well-educated nobleman, descended from Welsh Princes who, between 1400 and 1415, led a rebellion known since as 'the last Welsh revolt' or 'The Glyndŵr Rising'. Glyndŵr, a charismatic leader and military strategist, employed clever guerrilla-like tactics to release much of Wales from English control. His supporters hailed him the 'Prince of Wales', the last native Welshman to hold the title. His desire for independence and his plan for Wales were ambitious. He envisaged an independent parliament and church, two universities and a treaty with France. In 1405 Glyndŵr entered into the 'Tripartite indenture' – an agreement with Edmund Mortimer and Henry Percy, Earl of Northumberland, dividing England and Wales between them, using Merlinic prophecy in order to define the boundaries. Glyndŵr was to have Wales. Unfortunately, the uprising and the glorious plan for Wales was thwarted, and led by the future Henry V, the English re-gained control. Glyndŵr disappears in 1415, it is believed that he died, but the circumstances of his death and the location of his grave remain a mystery.

DID YOU KNOW?

- Blanche Parry (*c.* 1508–1509) a noble woman from Newcourt in Herefordshire attended Queen Elizabeth I since her birth in 1533. It is known that the Queen spoke at least seven languages and it is thought that Blanche may have taught her to speak Welsh.
- Welsh noblewoman Katheryn of Berain (*c.* 1535–1591) descendant of Henry VII is known as 'Mam Cymru' or the 'mother of Wales'. She was married four times, produced many children, giving rise to an incredibly far reaching network of descendants.

★ AMAZING FACT ★

GWENLLIAN AND THE GREAT REVOLT OF 1136
Wales was in bitter conflict with the invading Norman forces, and during the Great Revolt of 1136, Gwenllian (c. 1100 –1136) courageously led her husband the Prince of Deheubarth's army into battle, near Kidwelly Castle in Carmarthenshire. Gwenllian was defeated, captured and beheaded along with her two sons. This brave warrior Princess is regarded as the first woman to lead a Welsh army into battle; the site is still referred to as 'Maes Gwenllian'or 'Gwenllian's field.'

QUICK FACTS

It is said that poor Gwenllian's soul remains in torment; her ghost is sometimes seen to wander near the castle, still searching for her head!

DID YOU KNOW?

Merlin's Oak

An ancient prophecy declares 'When Merlin's oak shall tumble down, then shall fall Carmarthen town'. Carmarthen was Merlin's birthplace; an ancient oak tree known as 'Merlin's Oak', stood in the town for centuries. The oak was poisoned in the early 19th century, died in 1856 and in 1951 began to disintegrate. Despite protests from the townsfolk, the remains of the oak were removed in 1978; that year Carmarthen experienced some of the worst flooding ever recorded.

ANEURIN 'NYE' BEVAN (1897–1960)
The founding father of the National Health Service

Born in Tredegar, in Blaenau Gwent, Bevan left school aged 13 to take his turn working underground in a local colliery, where he became active in trade union politics. In 1918 he was awarded scholarship to the Central Labour College in London and in 1929 he took his place in the Houses of Parliament as MP of Ebbw Vale. Bevan became Minister of Health, following the landslide Labour victory in the 1945 general election, and took on his greatest political challenge; the founding of the National Health Service, which came into being on the 5 July 1948 in order to provide free healthcare at the point of delivery. In 1957 Bevan resigned from parliament as a protest at the introduction of prescription charges.

DAVID LLOYD GEORGE (1863–1945)
THE 'WELSH WIZARD'

Dynamic Liberal politician Lloyd George was Prime Minister from 1916 to 1922. He was of Welsh parentage, was brought up in Wales, spoke Welsh as a first language and is known to be the only Welsh speaking Prime minister, and also by the nickname 'The Welsh Wizard'. He is best known for mobilizing resources, galvanizing the war effort and leading Britain to victory in World War I. He was one of the 'Big Three' along with Georges Clemenceau of France and American President Woodrow Wilson, who negotiated the Treaty of Versailles with Germany in 1919 which brought the war to an end. He was made 1st Earl Lloyd George of Dwyfor in 1944.

EXTRAORDINARY FACT

LADY RHONDDA (1883–1958)

Margaret Haig Mackworth 2nd Viscountess Rhondda was an internationally successful business woman, political activist and Wales' most famous suffragette, who, despite her title, was not allowed to sit in the House of Lords. She campaigned against the ban which was finally lifted in 1958. She was the first woman to preside over the Institute of Directors. In her youth she spent a short time in prison for attempting to blow up a post box in Newport for the cause of women's suffrage, and in 1915 she miraculously survived the sinking of the RMS *Lusitania*.

Megan Lloyd George (1902–1966) politician, daughter of David Lloyd George and women's rights campaigner, became the first female MP for a Welsh constituency in 1929. In that year women over the age of 21 were allowed to vote for the first time in a General Election.

Frances Hoggan (1843–1927) from Brecon was the first woman in Britain to be awarded a medical degree.

Betsi Cadwaldr (1789–1860), often overlooked contemporary of Florence Nightingale during the Crimean war, campaigned tirelessly to improve conditions and the provision of health care to wounded servicemen.

Bertrand Russell (1872–1970) born in Trellech, Monmouthshire, was a philosopher, political activist, social critic and Nobel laureate, and was one of the founders of the Campaign for Nuclear Disarmament in 1957.

TOM JONES' TELEPHONE BOX
The voice from the valleys

Singer Sir Tom Jones, (1940– present), real name Tommy Woodward, is probably one of the most famous Welshmen *ever*! Born in Treforest, Mid Glamorgan, into a coal mining family, Jones rose to stardom in the 1960s with a string of hits, and has since gained fame all over the world. In 1978 he bought the red telephone box that stood on the corner of Laura Street near his home in Pontypridd – at that time no-one had

Tom Jones

phones in their houses so the public phone box was a shared facility. The phone box had a great significance to Tom as he spent hours in his youth on this phone talking to childhood sweetheart and future wife, Melinda. After purchasing the red telephone box he moved it to California, which had been his home since 1974.

Shirley Bassey (1937– present) is a world-famous singer from Tiger Bay, Cardiff, whose glittering career began in the 1950s. In 1959 her hit single *As I Love You* reached number one in the charts and stayed there for four weeks; the first Welsh artist to do so. She is best known as the voice of Bond film theme tunes *Goldfinger* (1964), *Diamonds are Forever* (1971) and *Moonraker* (1979).

QUICK FACTS

• Thomas Edward Lawrence (1888–1935) AKA *Lawrence of Arabia* was born in Tremadog, Caernarvonshire. He died of head injuries sustained as a result of a motor cycle accident. This tragic event led to the universal use of crash helmets.

• Henry Hughes Cooper is famous for being buried on two continents. A gravestone at Strata Florida Abbey in Cardiganshire bears the inscription 'The left leg and part of the thigh of Henry Hughes Cooper, was cut off and interr'd here, June 18, 1756'. He emigrated to America where the rest of his body was laid to rest.

QUICK FACTS

A remote 18th century cottage near Machynlleth called 'Bron-yr-Aur' or *'golden hill'* earned its place in music history as being the place where in 1970 the band Led Zeppelin wrote much of the material on their studio albums, *Led Zeppelin* III and *Led Zeppelin* IV. Tracks include *Immigrant Song* and *Stairway to Heaven*.

ARTHUR GRAHAM OWENS (1899–1957)
THE NAME'S OWENS, ARTHUR OWENS

During World War II, Arthur Owens, known Welsh Nationalist and ladies' man, acted as a double agent both for the allied forces and the German Intelligence agency 'Abwehr;' *Apparently his co-operation with the Germans was encouraged by the provision of attractive female company! Owens was one of the first agents to be involved in a counter-espionage operation called the* 'Double-Cross System' *or* 'XX System', *which fed false information*

Arthur Graham Owens

QUICK FACTS

• His MI5 codename was 'SNOW', while in Germany he was known as 'JOHNNY' or 'LORD JOHNNY'.

to German intelligence. 'Operation fortitude' is one such example that provided fake details regarding the locations of the D-Day landings. It has never been made clear exactly on which side Owens' allegiance lay.

EXTRAORDINARY FACT

GWEN FERCH ELLIS (c. 1542–1594)

Spinner and weaver from Denbigh, Gwen ferch Ellis was a well-known 'healer' and maker of protective 'charms'. Unfortunately, one of her charms was written down backwards, and when it was found in the home of local gentleman Thomas Mostyn, it was construed as an evil spell. Several witnesses gave evidence against her on counts of witchcraft and causing death and madness through her herbal treatments. In 1594 she was tried for witchcraft, found guilty and subsequently hanged. This was the first recorded trial and execution on such charges. It is said that she had been married three times, the first two gentlemen died within two years of their weddings, the third remains unaccounted for!

QUICK FACTS

Ruth Ellis (1926–1955) from Rhyl in Denbighshire, was the last woman to be hanged in Britain.

• Llewellyn Morris Humphreys, (1899–1965) AKA Murray *The Hump*, was a notorious Gangland mobster and racketeer of Welsh descent who operated alongside Al Capone in the *Chicago Outfit* in Chicago, Illinois during the Prohibition. Known as a smart businessman, Murray preferred to negotiate with cash instead of bullets. 'Hump' is said to be an abbreviation of his surname and a reference to Murray's liking for camel hair coats.

Llewellyn Morris Humphreys

• Howard Marks, (1945–2016) AKA *Mr Nice*, gained fame and notoriety for his extensive international drug smuggling operation and subsequent highly publicized court cases and custodial sentence. It is thought that he had links with MI6, the IRA, the Mafia and the CIA. Marks became an actor, musician, and author publishing an autobiography and anthology of drug stories and an examination of a distant relative, famous pirate Sir Henry Morgan, plus two thriller crime novels. In 1997 Marks stood for parliament advocating the legalization of cannabis.

EXTRAORDINARY FACT

WHAT IS IT ABOUT PORT TALBOT?

Port Talbot is an industrial town in the borough of Neath Port Talbot on the coast of South Wales. Nothing out of the ordinary there, but this town has produced an extraordinary wealth of acting talent. For example:

- Richard Burton (1925–1984) world famous giant of stage and screen, acclaimed for his incredible presence and famous 'voice', known for his narration of Dylan Thomas' radio play *Under Milkwood*.

- Ivor Emmanuel (1927–2007) best remembered for his rendition of 'Men of Harlech' in the 1964 film classic *Zulu*.

- Anthony Hopkins (1937–present) stage and screen actor, director and producer, most famous for his portrayal of Hannibal Lecter in psychological thriller *Silence of the Lambs* (1991).

- Michael Sheen (1969–present) RADA trained, Sheen first achieved recognition for stage performances, later better-known for his chameleon-like acting abilities and his spellbinding portrayals of real-life characters on screen. In 2011 he led a mammoth 72-hour performance of *The Passion*, beginning at the seafront at Aberafan in Port Talbot.

- Rob Brydon (1965–present) comedian, actor, singer, impressionist and star of radio and small screen.

QUICK FACTS

• Ray Milland (1929–1985) was the first Welsh actor to win an Academy Award for his role in *The Lost Weekend* (1945). He hailed from Neath which is near Port Talbot.

• Millicent Lilian 'Peg' Entwistle (1908–1932) emigrated to America from Port Talbot, to become a successful actress on Broadway. She achieved notoriety when she jumped to her death from the top of the letter 'H' in the Hollywood sign which at the time read 'Hollywoodland'.

DID YOU KNOW?

THE BAKED BEAN MUSEUM OF EXCELLENCE

A council flat in Port Talbot houses baked bean expert Captain Beany plus an eccentric and unique museum full of baked bean related artefacts. Back in 1986, Captain Beany formerly known as Barry Kirk, set a world record for sitting naked in a bathtub full of baked beans for 100 hours. Since then the Captain, clad in a golden superhero costume with his head painted orange, has continued to raise funds for charity.

HUB OF INDUSTRY

In the mid-18th century Wales was hailed as the world's first industrialized nation, though its history of mining stretches as far back as the Bronze Age. Industrialization brought prosperity for some and increased employment for thousands, but along with it an intense feeling of unrest within the workforce. This chapter explores industries throughout Welsh history.

THE GREAT ORME
Forgotten mines excavated using child labour

> **QUICK FACTS**
> There are approximately 8 km (5 miles) of tunnels in the mine system, some up to 70 m (230 ft) beneath the surface.

A fascinating 3,500-year-old copper mine lies beneath the headland known as the Great Orme near Llandudno in Conwy. Rediscovered in 1987, the mines are believed to be one of the largest Bronze Age mining complexes in Europe. Parts of the labyrinthine network of tunnels are so narrow that it is thought that only children would have been able to work there. Bronze Age miners would have used stone tools to reach the copper ore seams, then bone tools to extract the soft mineral known as 'Malachite' which was easily smelted. The resulting copper was a soft metal and useful for decorative purposes but not weaponry or tools, the addition of tin produced a harder substance known as bronze. Such an operation required a large, well organized skilled workforce, the communities surrounding the mines would have been sophisticated social units, able to communicate and trade with others close by and indeed as far as Europe. The mines were abandoned with the arrival of the Iron Age, then lay undisturbed until the 17th century when copper became a valuable commodity once again. The high-quality copper produced here was in great demand until the 1840s when the industry began its gradual decline; the mine was closed in 1918. There were many more copper mines across Wales but none on the scale of The Great Orme. Today it is a popular tourist destination.

AMAZING FACT

COPPEROPOLIS

Swansea was once the centre of the world's copper industry during the 18th and early 19th centuries, earning itself the name 'Copperopolis'. Copper was hugely popular at the time, used for everything from coins to cooking vessels, indeed, copper manufactured at Swansea and neighbouring town Llanelli, was used in the communication cables that carried the first messages along Transatlantic Cable Telegraph in 1866. The Royal Navy used copper sheathing to protect the hulls of its fleet, giving rise to the phrase 'copper-bottomed', meaning 'to be thoroughly reliable; certain not to fail'. Copperopolis is thought to have supplied about 70 per cent of the world's copper products at that time.

TINOPOLIS

Llanelli has been known historically as a mining town, but in the 18th and 19th centuries the growth of first the tinplate industry and later the steel works, gave rise to another nickname: 'Tinopolis'. It is thought that until the late 1800s, the majority of the world's tinplate was produced in Wales. Llanelli is also known for its large-scale production of tinplated cookware, earning Llanelli folk yet another nickname, the 'Sosbans'.

People from Swansea are called 'Jack' after the famous dog, but neighbouring folk from Llanelli are called 'Turks'; no-one knows for certain why!

ROMAN OCCUPATION
They came, they saw, they took the gold!

The Romans arrived in Wales in the year 48 AD primarily to exploit the rich mineral wealth that they knew to exist in the western reaches of Britain. They used their technical superiority, and plenty of Welsh slaves to mine for copper, lead, zinc and silver, but it was Welsh gold that was most prized, to be transformed into decorative artefacts and adornments for the wealthy. However, the extraction of the precious metal required deep mining, and even with Roman 'know how' the work required hard graft, using rudimentary hand tools in dreadful conditions underground. Welsh gold is extremely scarce today and there are no working mines.

DID YOU KNOW? The famous 'Mould Cape' found in 1833 is an extraordinarily intricate and beautiful ceremonial gold piece made by Welsh craftsmen in the early Bronze Age, about 3,700 years ago. The Welsh knew a thing or two about gold long before the Romans arrived!

★ AMAZING FACT ★

SLATE
Fine quality slate has been quarried in North Wales for nearly two millennia. The Romans recognized the advantages of slate as a building material, as did Edward I when he constructed Conwy Castle. However, the dawning of the Industrial Revolution in the 18th century saw a rapid increase in demand for slate in Britain and in Europe as industries and populations began to grow. During the 19th century demand outstripped supply and as alternative sources were found and this once thriving industry began to decline. Small scale slate production still exists in Wales today.

QUICK FACTS

• Penrhyn was considered the largest quarry in the world at the end of the 1800s and is still operational, while quarries at Llanberis and Blaenau Ffestiniog are now tourist attractions.

• A network of narrow gauge railways facilitated the transport of goods and materials. The great little railways of Wales that served miners and quarries such as The Blaenau Ffestiniog Railway are now popular tourist attractions.

QUICK FACTS

• Lead was used for water pipes and combined with tin to make pewter tableware. Silver made fine tableware and coinage.

• Dolaucothi Gold Mines in Carmarthenshire are the oldest in Wales. First excavations are thought to be about 74 AD. The mine was closed in 1938.

• The Clogau Gold Mine near Dolgellau produced about 165 tons of gold ore between 1862–1911, known as the 'Gold Rush Period'. In the 1990s gold extraction cost an astonishing £1,000 an ounce. Welsh gold has been used to make wedding rings for the British Royal Family since 1923.

BLACK GOLD
The world's first industrialized nation

More people were employed in heavy industry in Wales by 1850 than in agriculture and rural occupations; thus Wales emerged as the world's first industrialized nation. The Welsh were no strangers to mining the history of which can be traced back for millennia. Mining on a small scale existed from the 15th through to the 17th centuries, but extraction of the valuable coal deposits on an industrial scale began in earnest during the 18th century. Wales' black gold was the fuel that drove the Industrial Revolution. Rapid expansion followed, and by 1913, there were more than 600 mines in operation supporting a work force in excess of 230,000 men. Output was phenomenal, coal exports from Barry in the Vale of Glamorgan were the largest in the world. However, World War I brought political and economic change, the depression that followed, combined with increased use of oil as a fuel source and the rise in competition from overseas coal producers, drove the industry into a decline. The coal industry was nationalized in 1947. A series of pit closures during the 1980s sanctioned by a government led by Margaret Thatcher culminated in major industrial action and the miner's strike in 1984–85 led by Arthur Scargill of the National Union of Mineworkers. This was the beginning of the end for the coal industry. We should never forget that while industrialization brought prosperity and employment, transforming both the landscape and society, it brought with it hardship and heartbreak. Numerous tragic incidents throughout the coal industry's history caused many thousands of families to pay the terrible price of coal. The disaster at Senghenydd colliery

in 1913 that killed 439 miners and the tragedy at Aberfan in 1966 that took the lives of 116 children and 28 adults have come to symbolize the tyranny of the coal industry.

AMAZING FACT

Rapid industrialization between 1760–1914 gave rise to an increased demand for labour. It is thought that two thirds of the population migrated from rural areas of Wales to the growing towns in the industrialized south.

QUICK FACTS

• The first million pound deal was struck at Cardiff's Coal Exchange in 1904. Disappointingly there is no evidence to support the popular claim that the first cheque for that amount was signed at the same time.

• Blaenavaon Collliery, in the South Wales Valleys, was operational from 1880–1980 and opened to the public in 1983. The 'Big Pit' National Coal Museum is an UNESCO World Heritage site, offering the visitor an extraordinary experience of life underground.

LUCY THOMAS (1781–1847) INDUSTRIALIST

Swansea born Lucy Thomas took over her husband's colliery after his death in 1833; a radical move for a woman in those days when industry was largely dominated by men, moreover it was a great achievement for Lucy as she was illiterate. The deals Lucy struck with merchants in London helped to establish the reputation of the Welsh coal industry, earning her the title *'The mother of the steam coal industry'*.

LITTLE HELL
Farming village becomes the 'Iron Capital of the World'

The Industrial Revolution transformed Merthyr, in mid-Glamorgan, from little more than a sleepy farming town in 1760 into the iron capital of the world within the space of a few decades due to its proximity to natural reserves of iron ore and coal. Ironworks sprung up all over the Merthyr area, providing materials for the expanding railway and shipbuilding industries, causing an influx of labour from both Wales and Britain. The sudden increase in population and a shortage of accommodation gave rise to squalid overcrowded slum areas, one in particular was known as 'China' or 'Little Hell'. The inhabitants known as 'Chinese' were desperately poor, and endured the most appalling living conditions in Britain. Families crowded into tiny hovels on narrow streets with no sanitation; a breeding ground for diseases such as cholera and typhoid and infestations of lice. Lawlessness and criminal activity were rife, street gangs proliferated in an unrelenting environment of misery, hunger and squalor.

QUICK FACTS

It was during the Merthyr Rising that the red flag was first raised as a symbol of protest and solidarity.

DID YOU KNOW?

HUGHESOVKA

John Hughes (1814–1889) industrialist and ironmaster from Cyfarthfa in South Wales, migrated to Russia in 1870 along with about 100 iron workers and their families. He established collieries and iron works supplying iron for the railways that would span the Russian Empire. He built a new town in the Ukraine called 'Hughesovka, known since 1961 as Donetsk.

EXTRAORDINARY FACT

DIC PENDERYN (1808–1831)

The Merthyr Rising took place in June 1831, where thousands of miners and iron workers took to the streets of Merthyr Tydfil to protest against redundancies, wage reductions and rising prices. Several days of violent protest followed, armed soldiers were sent to quash the uprising, resulting in many deaths. Richard Lewis AKA *Dic Penderyn*, was a miner accused of stabbing a soldier during the riot. A petition protesting his innocence containing the signatures of 11,000 local people was unsuccessful. He was hanged on the 13 August but was hailed a hero and the first working-class martyr. Some years later it was discovered that another individual, one Ianto Parker, had committed the crime and had subsequently left the country.

THE PENYDARREN LOCO
Who was the real father of the railways?

On the 21 February 1804 a steam locomotive designed by Cornish mining engineer Richard Trevithick (1771–1833) made the world's first steam powered journey on the rails of the tramway from Penydarren Ironworks to the Merthyr–Cardiff canal. The Penydarren Locomotive travelled a distance of 14.4 km (9 miles), hauling 10 tons of iron in 5 wagons, plus 70 men sitting on top of the iron. This extraordinary achievement preceded George Stephenson's much publicized journey by several years, thus giving rise to the opinion that Trevithick was indeed the true father of the railways. Steam locomotion soon became commercially viable and by the end of the century rail networks were operating worldwide.

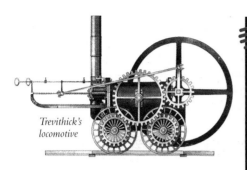

Trevithick's
locomotive

MUMBLES RAILWAY
PIONEERS OF FEE-PAYING PASSENGER TRAVEL

*The Mumbles railway was first used in 1804 to haul materials by
horse-drawn tram from the mines and quarries in Mumbles along
the coast of Swansea Bay to the dockyards at Swansea. There was no
road so the only alternative had been to take the materials by boat
across the bay. An act of parliament gave permission for mechanical
power to be used in addition to horses to draw wagons along the
8 km (5 mile) track. However, history was made on the 25 March
1807, when a converted carriage transported the world's first fee
paying railway passengers along the same route. The service became
most popular with people who could afford to pay the shilling for the
fare. The railway continued to use horses up until 1896, though it is
known that steam powered carriages were introduced in 1877. For a*

*time, permission was given for two
companies to operate on the line
simultaneously, one used steam
locomotives and the other horse
power! The railway was returned*

to a single operator at the end of the century and in 1902 attempted unsuccessfully to use battery-powered accumulator cars. Between 1900 and 1920 the service used very large passenger carriages, often carrying 1,800 passengers in a single trip. Steam eventually gave way to tramcars powered by overhead electric cables in 1929 which were operational until the railways closure in 1960.

EXTRAORDINARY FACT

In the very early days of the Mumbles railway an experiment was conducted to explore the possibility of using wind power as an alternative method of traction to horses. A sail was duly rigged to a carriage, and with the aid of a strong following wind, the journey time was reduced to 45 minutes. However, the idea was abandoned in favour of more reliable methods.

REBECCA AND HER DAUGHTERS
Men disguised as women storm the toll gates of Wales

The Rebecca Riots occurred across rural parts of West Wales between 1839 and 1843, initiated by tenant farmers and farm workers in protest against the introduction

of toll charges for the transportation of animals and goods on the roads, which were largely privately owned by Turnpike Trusts. Due to adverse weather condition and crop failures, the agricultural communities were poverty stricken; tolls were the last straw. Gangs of men disguised in women's clothing, with masked or blackened faces calling themselves 'Rebecca and her Daughters' stormed and destroyed many toll gates, which had come to represent the oppressive and unfair system. The 'Rebeccas' would sometimes carry out a mock trial preceding the attacks. The name is derived from a passage in The Bible relating to Rebekah that reads '*let thy seed possess the gate of those which hate them*' (Genesis XXIV, verse 60). By 1844 an act of parliament was passed amending the laws relating to the Turnpike Trusts. Rebecca was never seen again!

EXTRAORDINARY FACT

THE LAST READING OF THE RIOT ACT

The first ever railway strike took place on the 17 August 1911 in Llanelli, Carmarthenshire in protest against poor wages and working conditions. Railway and tinplate workers formed blockades at two railway crossings to stop all traffic on what was then the main route between England and Ireland. Several hundred armed troops from The Worcestershire Regiment were dispatched to the town, the riot act was read and two young men were shot and killed. Several days of rioting followed before a settlement was negotiated.

THE RIOT ACT.

If any persons to the number of 12 or more unlawfully, riotously, and tumultuously assemble together to the disturbance of the public peace and being required by any Justice by proclamation in the King's name in the exact form of the Riot Act, I George I, Sess. 2 a 5 x 2, to disperse themselves and peaceably depart, shall to the number of 12 or more unlawfully, riotously and tumultuously remain or continue together for an hour after such proclamation shall be guilty of a felony.

The Form of Proclamation is as follows:—

"Our Sovereign Lord the King chargeth and commandeth all persons being assembled, immediately to disperse themselves, and peaceably depart to their habitations, or to their lawful business, upon the pains contained in the Act made in the first year of King George the First for preventing tumults and riotous assemblies.-"

GOD SAVE THE KING.

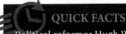

QUICK FACTS

Political reformer Hugh Williams (1796–1874) established the Chartist movement in Carmarthen in 1836, calling for electoral and parliamentary reforms and universal suffrage for men.

The 3-year long strike at Penrhyn State Quarry began in 1900 and is known as the longest industrial dispute in British History.

The Tony Pandy Riots (1910–1911) were a series of violent clashes between striking coal miners and the police in the Rhondda in an attempt to persuade the mining Cartels to improve wages.

On the 5 September 1911 the pupils at Bigyn School, Llanelli, left their classrooms and marched through the town in protest against the use of the cane. This prompted a series of similar protests across Britain.

The Carmarthen Cheese Riot erupted on the 25 September 1818. Angry crowds blocked a shipment of cheese out of Carmarthen dock. Cheese had become a vital staple and a substitute for meat for the townsfolk; their protest was against the export of cheese as opposed to local distribution.

The Newport Rising on the 4 September 1839 was a violent armed protest led by John Frost (1784–1877). Thousands of angry protesters demanded the release of fellow chartist Henry Vincent from prison. Troops were summoned and more than 20 rioters were shot and killed and many more injured. Leaders of the rising were convicted of treason and sentenced to death, later commuted to transportation. John Frost was pardoned in 1856 and subsequently hailed a hero.

WOMEN'S ROLE IN A DANGEROUS INDUSTRY

A peaceful country park's hidden history

The undulating sand dunes of Pembrey Burrows that now form part of Pembrey Country Park in Carmarthenshire hide an explosive past. In 1882 the Stowmarket Explosives Company began the manufacture of dynamite for use in the mines and quarries in the safety of the dunes. This was extremely dangerous work and production came to a halt after an explosion took the lives of seven workers, the youngest was only 13. The beginning of World War I saw a new factory on the site, making explosives and munitions which were transported by rail and sea to the battlefields in Europe and the Middle East. The factory employed a huge workforce of 6,000 local people, mostly women. When the war came to an end the factory was dismantled, but in 1938 the threat of World War II prompted the building of The Royal Ordnance Factory at Pembrey, one of only four manufacturers in the whole of Britain to produce TNT. By 1964 production ceased altogether and the plant was closed.

Women formed a major part of the hazardous and dangerous munitions industry during wartime, freeing men to join the Armed Forces. Exposure to TNT caused poisoning which resulted in a yellow discolouration of the skin. Women workers were often referred to as 'Canaries'.

OUTNUMBERED 3:1

There are in excess of 9 million sheep in Wales, outnumbering people 3:1 at the last count. Sheep farming has been an important industry in Wales for centuries, although it is thought that the characteristic white fluffy variety that we know today was probably imported by the Romans. By 1660, wool accounted for an astonishing two-thirds of Wales' exports. The arrival of the power loom in 1850 accelerated production but the industry had all but disappeared in the 20th century, and today only a handful of working woollen mills remain.

QUICK FACTS

The Brynmawr Experiment (1923–1940) was a successful furniture making enterprise undertaken by the Quaker community in 1929, as a solution to mass unemployment in the small town of Brynmawr in Brecknockshire.

EXTRAORDINARY FACT

THE CORACLE 'Y Cwrgwl'

These strange oval shaped one-man boats have been used for many centuries for fishing on rivers and streams and are particularly associated with Wales. Made from woven willow rods and covered with animal skin sealed with tar, the coracle is lightweight, portable, waterproof and looks rather like half a walnut shell or a shallow bowl. Traditionally coracles were used in pairs with a fishing net suspended between; or used singly for pole or line fishing. A coracle is paddled using one oar in a figure of 8 pattern from the front, the flat-bottomed shape was very stable and well suited for use in shallow waters. They were often used at night for poaching as they floated silently in the water and were almost invisible in the dark. Up until the late 1960s coracles were used to help wash sheep. Coracle men would use the boats to guide the sheep as they swam across the River Teifi at 'flat rock' below the bridge at Cenarth. The sheep were then driven back across the bridge and the process was repeated twice more. Cleaner wool fetched a better price at the market. In addition to fishing, coracles have been used as a mode of transport, a postal service, a rescue boat for people and livestock stranded in flood water, and much more. A coracle used for fishing is a rare sight today. The Salmon and Freshwater Fisheries Act 1923 abolished coracle fishing on many Welsh rivers, and today the practice is limited to a handful of licence holders on the Towy Teifi and the Taf.

QUICK FACTS

• In July 1974 Welshman Bernard Thomas (1923–2014) coracle maker and vice president of The Coracle Society crossed the English Channel in a Teifi coracle; the journey took 13 and a half hours.

FUN AND GAMES

If you thought that rugby was a tough game, think again. Ancient and traditional Welsh sports had no rules, no restrictions and sometimes no clothes! Wales is well known for its sporting prowess, especially rugby, but here are some unusual facts about sporting and leisure activities enjoyed by thrill seekers of yesteryear and adrenaline junkies of today.

CNAPAN, BANDO, AND PÊL-LAW
Ancient games without frontiers (or rules)

Cnapan was a form of medieval football, associated with West Wales. Welsh historian George Owen of Henllys (1552–1613) describes how teams of men often numbering several hundred, from two neighbouring villages or parishes, competed to gain possession of a small oiled wooden ball; the aim was to return the ball to the teams' home village or parish, by fair means or foul. There were no rules as such and usually teams played naked, as clothes would usually be ripped off during the course of the 'game'. Play was occasionally interrupted by the cry '*heddwch*' or 'peace' in order to restore order. Cnapan can be seen as the forerunner for rugby and association football, but gradually fell into decline as the modern games gained popularity.

Bando was an 18th century sport played between two teams of about 30 players, each wielding a curved wooden club resembling a hockey stick, called a 'bando'. The game is similar in style to shinty or hockey and formal rules and restrictions are few. Bando was a popular pastime amongst competitive, boisterous young men throughout Wales until the end of the 19th century. The game was an extremely popular spectator sport, and eventually the combination of alcohol, gambling, and violent behaviour on and off the pitch drove bando into obscurity. However, more recently the game has seen a modest revival where it is played as part of Easter celebrations in some parts of Wales.

Pêl-law or 'hand ball' is thought to be Wales' first national sport, as there is evidence of play since the middle ages. The walls of buildings were used until purpose built courts were constructed in the 18th century. The rules are similar to squash, but played with the hand and not a raquet. During the Tudor period between 1485 and 1603 many sports were banned in Wales by the English Crown as such activities were seen to be a distraction from more useful practices like archery, as the Welsh were known and valued for their skills with the longbow. However, Pêl-law continued to be played by Welsh people almost as a protest. By the 19th century, industrial development gave rise to a sharp increase in the working population in Wales, and the popularity of Pêl-law as a participation and a spectator sport rose accordingly, only to decline again in the 20th centrury. During the Depression in the 1930s street versions of the game continued, as a form of free entertainment for the poor and unemployed.

WEIRD SPORTS
Snorkel saves Victorian spa town

L lanwrtyd Wells in Powys, hailed as the smallest town
in Britain, was a thriving spa destination for Victorian
health tourists until the early 20th century. Unable to rely on
farming alone, enterprising locals decided to invent a new
'attraction' to boost trade and encourage visitors to return, and
in 1976 'Bog Snorkelling' put Llanwrtyd Wells back on the
tourist map. This extraordinary activity requires contestants to
complete two lengths of a 55 m (60 yard) long water-logged
peat bog trench, as fast as possible, using a snorkel and flippers
(fancy dress is encouraged). Neil Rutter set the world record
at 1 minute 18.8 seconds in 2018. The World Bog Snorkelling
Championships have been held in Llanwrtyd every year since
1985. The weirdness does not stop there, in 1980, there was
a bet in a pub that a man was equal to a horse. The Man vs
Horse race is now held every year in June, where runners race
against riders over a gruelling 35 km (22 mile) course. And
if that's not enough, in 2012 Llanwrtyd upped their game
and held the first World Alternative Games, which included
stone skimming, worm charming, and finger jousting, not to
mention wife carrying, husband dragging,
backward running and space hopper
races, then there's gravy wrestling
and Russian egg roulette and
much, much more. The event is
held every other year, and runs for
17 days in August.

DID YOU KNOW?

In 1732 the Rev. Theophilus Evans famously claimed that the healing properties of the water produced at the Dol-y-Coed Well had cured his scurvy. Llanwrtyd Wells thus became a popular spa town, however the spa itself was referred to as 'Ffynnon Ddrewllyd' or 'Stinking Well', due to the strong smell of hydrogen sulphide.

EXTRAORDINARY FACT

'Race the train' is a cross country running event held annually in Tywyn, Merionethshire. The aim of the race is to attempt to beat a steam train on the historic Talyllyn Railway over its journey from Talyllyn to Abergynolwyn and back; a distance of 22.5 km (14 miles).

LLANELLI 9 – NEW ZEALAND 3
The famous day the pubs ran dry

On the 31 October 1972 Llanelli's rugby team, the Scarlets, beat the New Zealand All Blacks touring side 9 – 3, becoming one of a few club teams to do so. The crowd at Stradey Park rugby ground was 25,000 strong that day; a day that will be remembered as one of the most important moments in Welsh sporting history. Upon hearing the news of the victory, one Llanelli policeman issued a warning to two afternoon shoppers, 'Ladies you'd better go home quick…

QUICK FACTS

'I was there' is a proud claim of all that attended the game that day. Though over the years many thousands more claim that they were 'there' too. The capacity of Stradey Park has increased retrospectively over the years!

the Scarlets have just beaten the All Blacks. All hell is going to break loose!' Grown men wept as their hearts filled with pride, Stradey Park spilled out onto the streets of Llanelli and the jubilant supporters drank the town's pubs dry.

DID YOU KNOW?

RUGBY IS WALES' NATIONAL SPORT

In 1905 at Cardiff Arms Park, Wales beat the New Zealand 'colonial' team 3 - 0 and were unofficially recognized as 'champions of the world'. It was at this game that the Welsh National Anthem was first sung at a sporting event.

When Wales defeated Ireland in the first Grand Slam tournament in 1908, they did so wearing their trial jerseys that did not bear the Prince of Wales feather emblem because someone had packed the wrong kit!

Richard Mullock (1851–1920) is credited with the establishment of Welsh Rugby Union in 1881 and organizing the first International rugby union match between Wales and England in that year.

AMAZING FACT

A RUGBY WORLD CUP TRADITION

In 1905 Welshman Gil Evans refereed the first test match between the All Blacks and England. Evans gave his whistle to referee Albert Freethy, who used it for the next twenty years. The famous whistle was donated to the New Zealand Rugby Museum in 1969. In 1987 Gil Evans' Welsh whistle was used to start the Rugby World Cup, and has been used at the first game of the World Cup every year since.

QUICK FACTS

• On the 23 April 1927 Cardiff City beat Arsenal 1 - 0 at Wembley Stadium, thus becoming the only non-English football team to win the FA Cup.

• Cardiff City began life as a cricket club. The players formed a football team in order to keep fit during the winter months. The club was founded in 1899 as Riverside A.F.C. as a way of keeping players from the Riverside Cricket Club together and in shape during the winter months.

• Swansea City Football Club were the first Welsh team to win promotion to the English Premier league in 2011.

THE GREAT ORME TRAMWAY
Day trippers share their journey with a coffin

The Great Orme Tramway was opened in 1902 and is an extraordinary mode of transport in the popular seaside town of Llandudno, North Wales. It is the last cable-operated tramway in Britain and one of a handful that survive worldwide. The route is in two sections – the lower part is a street running funicular line, while the upper part is an independent funicular. Passengers are required to change cars at the halfway point on their journey from Llandudno Victoria Station near Llandudno's famous pier, to the glorious summit of the Great Orme 207 m (670 ft) above in order to enjoy spectacular views.

Originally the tramway was used to carry goods and foot passengers, however the service was also utilized to carry coffins and mourners up to St Tudno's chapel, situated near the Halfway Station.

Mourners paid standard price for their tickets and the coffin was extra.

★ AMAZING FACT ★

THE ABERYSTWYTH CLIFF RAILWAY

Opened in 1896, it is the second longest funicular railway in Britain. The railway first operated on a water balance system until electrification in 1921, and rises 237.1 m (778 ft) from the promenade to the top of Constitution Hill above. The railway was used to take fun loving Victorian tourists from the arcades and restaurants along the seafront up to the Camera Obscura and recreational area at the top of the hill, where visitors could, on a clear day, see 26 Welsh mountain peaks. The railway remains a popular tourist attraction.

St Tudno's chapel

QUICK FACTS

'ALL SHOOK UP' IN PORTHCAWL
Every September since 2004 the small seaside town of Porthcawl in South Wales hosts one of the world's biggest Elvis festivals. For one weekend, more than 35,000 devoted fans, tribute acts and performers from all over the world gather to pay homage to the 'King of Rock and Roll'.

The Machynlleth Loop, AKA the *Mach Loop*, is a series of valleys in west-central Wales, between Dolgellau and Machynlleth, used by RAF jet aircraft for low level training exercises. It is unique to Wales and one of the few places worldwide that keen photographers and thrill seekers can climb to a mountain top and see jet aircraft in flight below; close enough at times to wave to the pilots.

ARTHUR LINTON (1868–1896)

Welsh lad got on his bike and became Champion Cyclist of the World

A phenomenon occurred in the Cynon Valley in the 1890s. The Aberdare Bicycle Club in Glamorganshire produced no fewer than four world-class racing cyclists; namely Arthur Linton and his brothers Tom and Samuel, together with Jimmy Michael, Arthur's principle rival. Arthur Linton achieved much local and international success and in

1894 beat the French champion to win the title 'Champion Cyclist of the World'. Linton's death 6 weeks after his triumph in the Bordeaux to Paris Race in 1896 brought the extraordinary cyclist's brief but glittering career to an end. In the years that followed, speculation arose that his death was caused by drug use or 'doping' after fellow rider Jimmy Michael was banned from racing in Britain amidst suspicions of taking performance enhancing drugs. It was thought that manager 'Choppy' Warburton was responsible for providing the mysterious concoctions in 'little black bottles' to revive his riders.

Arthur Linton, Choppy Warburton, Jimmy Michael, Tom Linton

EXTRAORDINARY FACT

During the 1860s, Wrexham born inventor Major Walter Clopton Wingfield (1833–1912) invented a lawn version of the indoor game 'real tennis', after playing with a ball that was designed to bounce on grass. He called the new game 'Sphairistike', loosely derived from a Greek word for 'ball game'. The Major developed his idea, formalized a set of rules then patented his new game. In 1874 he began marketing boxed 'Sphairistike' sets containing equipment, instructions and a vulcanized rubber ball. Lawn tennis as a leisure pursuit caught on very quickly, however the name 'Sphairistike' did not!

Lake Snowdonia

ADRENALINE JUNKIES' PARADISE
• The National White Water Rafting Centre offers exhilarating white water experiences on the rapids of the River Tryweryn within the glorious surroundings of Snowdonia National Park. Not for the faint hearted!

• The Penrhyn Slate Quarry in North Wales boasts the fastest zip line in the world and the longest in Europe. It is possible to travel at more than 160.9 km per hour (100 miles per hour).

• The Fforest Coaster in Betws y Coed, in Conwy, stretches for half a mile through beautiful Snowdonia woodland; an interesting twist on a fairground favourite. The gravity driven roller coaster can reach speeds of 40 km per hour (25 miles per hour), if you're brave enough to not use the brakes.

• Combine caving with trampolining deep inside the disused Llechwedd Slate Caverns that are the size of St Paul's Cathedral in Blaenau Ffestiniog.

• Extreme camping in Holy Island, Anglesey – you can, if you are totally fearless, spend the night strapped into a camp bed, dangling from a cliff edge, 15 m (50 ft) above the sea below.

Mount Everest is named after Sir George Everest (1790–1866) from Crickhowell in Powys, who was Surveyor General of India. Sadly, he never saw the mountain that bears his name.

INDEX

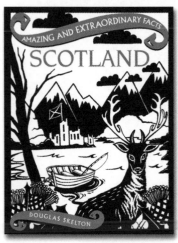

Amazing and Extraordinary
Facts: Scotland
Douglas Skelton
ISBN: 978-1-910821-14-5

Amazing and Extraordinary
Facts: Great Britain
Stephen Halliday
ISBN: 978-1-910821-20-6

Amazing and Extraordinary
Facts: Prime Ministers
Jonathan Bastable
ISBN: 978-1-910821-22-0

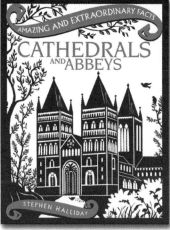

Amazing and Extraordinary
Facts: Cathedrals and Abbeys
Stephen Halliday
ISBN: 978-1-910821-04-6

For more great books visit our website at **www.rydonpublishing.co.uk**

THE AUTHOR

Alison Jenkins is a creative designer, maker and author who hails from Llanelli in South Wales, and has a special interest in all things Welsh. Her initial training in fashion design and illustration took her away from the homeland to London where she became a regular contributor to leading women's interest publications before venturing into the world of books. She is author of many titles that have been published worldwide on an extraordinary variety of subjects ranging from DIY, home style and specialized crafts, through to fancy dress for dogs and Towel Origami! Alison now lives and works in East Anglia.

AUTHOR ACKNOWLEDGEMENTS

Many thanks to Adrian for your support and to my parents Mavis and Howell for the stories!

PICTURE CREDITS

Pages 21, 25, 27, 29, 34, 53, 58, 59, 61, 63, 74, 79, 91, 94, 96, 97, 109, 126, 127, 134 courtesy of the British Library Flickr collection.
Pg 105 adapted from work (Wikimedia UK) under license CC BY-SA 4.0